FREE *at* LAST

FREE *at* LAST

Experiencing True Freedom Through Your Identity In Christ

TONY EVANS

MOODY PRESS
CHICAGO

ISBN 0-8024-8580-4
Printed in the United States of America

To Kirk Franklin,
my spiritual son,
who continues to grow in grace
and the knowledge of his identity in Christ

CONTENTS

WITH GRATITUDE

I want to say a word of thanks to my friend and editor, Philip Rawley, for his excellent help in the preparation of this manuscript; and to Greg Thornton, Cheryl Dunlop, and the rest of the team at Moody Press for their encouragement and quality work on this project.

INTRODUCTION

Far too many Christians are stuck in spiritual quicksand. The harder they struggle to progress in their walk with Christ, the faster and the deeper they appear to sink.

Having become frustrated by the inability of their increased efforts to produce the joy, peace, power, and victory they have heard so much about, many believers have simply given up the struggle and have allowed themselves to sink in the quicksand of spiritual defeat, accepting it as their lot in life.

These well-meaning saints go to church faithfully and attend every Christian conference they can find. They read Christian books, listen to Christian radio, and watch Christian television. They dedicate and rededicate their lives to the Lord until they are tired of walking the aisle, crying and begging God for help. Some have fasted and prayed and even sought Christian counseling to deal with their frustration, yet there seems to be little payoff for their efforts.

Some of these saints are stuck in sins and circumstances they know they should be delivered from, but while they wholeheartedly desire deliverance, it continues to elude them.

If you can identify with any of the conditions described above, this book is for you. It is written for sincere Christians who are sick and tired of enduring the agony of defeat and want to taste the thrill of victory instead. This book is designed to help those who feel they have to keep up appearances and speak the language of spiritual victory, all the while knowing they are living under a cloud of failure.

My thesis for this book is quite simple: If you have a heart that desperately desires to know and serve God, the place to begin is by understanding and *believing* the biblical truth of your identity in Christ. This is a watershed issue, one that determines whether you will live free in Christ or live as a slave of the world, the flesh, and the devil.

I consider the truth about our identity in Christ to be the greatest principle of Christian living in Scripture. As I seek to unfold this truth in the pages to come, it is my hope that it will become the key to unlock and release you from the shackles of whatever may be holding you hostage.

Chapter One

IT'S TIME FOR YOUR LIBERATION

A special lady stands in New York Harbor. She's called "Lady Liberty," the Statue of Liberty, a symbol of freedom for the whole world. Everything about this great statue speaks of freedom. The poet Emma Lazarus wrote the famous poem found on the pedestal, which invites the world to bring its "huddled masses yearning to breathe free" to these shores.

The lady holds high a lamp to light the way for those seeking freedom. Her crown has seven points beckoning to the seven seas and the seven continents, inviting every part of the earth to bring their oppressed to America. The tablet in her hand is inscribed with the date of the Declaration of Independence. And at her feet lies a chain representing tyranny that has been broken.

This image of freedom reaching out to those in bondage beckons to the people of God in this age, because many among us are in bondage.

I believe God is holding high the lamp of His Word and saying, "Bring Me your pain, your depression, your guilt, your failure, your discouragement, and your addictions. Bring Me your broken homes, your rebellious children, and your messed-up marriages. Bring Me your sin and your circumstances, from every ocean or continent of your existence."

God is calling His people to break the chains of tyranny because bondage is totally incongruous with our life in Jesus Christ—the One who said, "You will know the truth, and the truth will make you free," and "If therefore the Son makes you free, you will be free indeed" (John 8:32, 36).

The thesis of this book is very simple: God wants to set His people free. I'm not talking about salvation here, because this book is addressed primarily to Christians. By freedom I mean being free from anyone or anything other than Christ that is controlling your life. Free from the need to pop that pill, take that drink, look at that pornography, buy that lottery ticket, or do anything else to deaden the pain of a life held in spiritual bondage.

Therefore, my goal for this book is also simple. I hope, by the power of the Holy Spirit's illuminating ministry, to light a lamp and hold it up to God's Word. My prayer is that as you understand and apply the truth of who you are in Jesus Christ, you will be liberated. Chains will lie broken at your feet.

That's a tall order, which is why only God can do it. But I have accepted the challenge of discovering biblical freedom, and so I say bring your need to the foot of the cross, where chains are broken. You can enjoy a new freedom in your daily Christian life.

THE REALITY OF SPIRITUAL BONDAGE

Why is it that we try so hard and don't go very far in our spiritual lives? Why do we leave church Sunday on a spiritual high, only to return to the pits on Monday? And why, at other times, do we do the very things we don't want to do? What is holding us hostage to problems like these?

These issues, and a host of others like them, speak to the reality of spiritual bondage. Most people who are being held captive want to be set free. But in order to be set free, a person must first realize that he is in bondage. In order to break the chains that hold us, we must understand who put those chains on us and how they got there in the first place.

I want to go to a passage of Scripture that addresses this root issue. The apostle Paul wrote to the believers at Corinth, "I am afraid that, as the serpent deceived Eve by his craftiness, your minds will be led astray from the simplicity and purity of devotion to Christ" (2 Corinthians 11:3).

Paul knew that the same crafty serpent that had duped Eve in the Garden of Eden was messing with the Corinthians' minds. What scared Paul was not that the serpent was in control of their circumstances, but that he was in their heads. He had coiled himself around their thinking processes and their emotions.

Now that's bad because we're talking about "the serpent of old who is called the devil and Satan, who deceives the whole world" (Revelation 12:9). If Satan ever coils himself around your mind, there aren't enough pills in the world that you can take to fix the problem. There is no number of seminars you can attend, or vacations you can take, to get free if he's messing with your mind. Paul said the Corinthians were being deceived.

The Deceiver's Work

What is the nature of Satan's deception? What is this trickery he has brought about? Paul pointed his readers back to Satan's deception of Eve—but he didn't bring up Eve just to teach a history or a theology lesson.

Paul was saying to his spiritual children at Corinth, "Understand what the deceiver did to Eve, and you'll understand what he's trying to do to you." That's what the Holy Spirit is saying to us too. What happened to Eve is important because the serpent is still hissing today, thousands of years later.

Since this is true, we need to review the temptation that plunged first Eve and then Adam into sin. I also want to talk about the results of their sin, because in this we can trace the roots of the problems Christians struggle with today.

You'll recall God's prohibition against eating any fruit from the Tree of the Knowledge of Good and Evil (Genesis 2:17). When the serpent came to Eve, this was the issue he wanted to discuss with her (3:1–3).

Eve knew exactly what God had commanded, but then the serpent hit her with this: "You surely will not die! For God knows that in the day you eat from it [the forbidden tree] your eyes will be opened, and you will be like God, knowing good and evil" (Genesis 3:4–5).

The deception worked. Being like God had a nice ring to it for Eve. She not only ate the fruit, but she served some to Adam and he ate it too (v. 6). And God's judgment fell on them.

Satan used the same temptation on Eve that he himself had fallen for when he was in heaven—the desire to be independent of God, to be self-sufficient, to be his own god. Five times in Isaiah 14:13–14, Satan had said, "I will . . ." Now he was saying to Eve, "You can . . ." We could call this the sin of self-sufficiency.

Satan's reply to Eve planted his own evil thoughts in her mind. "Eat this fruit, and you'll be as wise as God. You'll have His knowledge base. He doesn't want that because He's jealous of you. But you don't need God. You can do it yourself. This can be your Independence Day from God!"

"Do-It-Yourself" Christianity

We live in a do-it-yourself world, but I hate going to our local "handyman" store. It's part of a large national chain of such stores, and one reason I don't like it is because of those endless, huge aisles. I can never seem to find the item I need.

But the real reason I don't like going to this particular store is that it means I have something I've got to do myself. Something at home needs either to be fixed or installed. And I have to come up with a way to get the job done because stores like this have empowered people to think they can do it themselves.

Why call a plumber or an electrician when you can buy all the plumbing or electrical stuff you need and do the job yourself? Just roam those big aisles at the handyman store long enough, and you'll find the materials to do anything.

The problem with many of us is that we have transferred this same kind of thinking to our Christian lives. We have become so used to doing it ourselves that, although we know Jesus said we can't do anything apart from Him (John 15:5), we've just been self-sufficient for too long.

We may have the right spiritual verbiage, but self takes over and soon we are trying to be like the "Most High," which was Satan's original sin. That's why he wants to get us operating independently of God.

Satan's goal is to keep sinners from going to heaven and to keep saints from enjoying the trip to heaven by tying them up in spiritual bondage and defeat. When a Christian lives in perpetual defeat, Satan wins. Every time the Enemy gets us in a position where our lifestyle contradicts what God says is true, he wins by deception.

Confusing Your Identity

Of all the tricks Satan has in his bag to promote self-sufficiency and independence from God, he has one that's a favorite because it is so effective. Satan wants to keep you spiritually off balance and defeated by confusing your identity.

The devil wants sinners to think they're saints and saints to think they're sinners. If he can confuse your identity, you won't know who you are, and once that happens you won't know how to act.

I've been learning to use a computer, which is a real surprise to the people who know me. I've learned enough to know that you need a device called an emulator to run otherwise incompatible programs on the same computer.

The emulator can make one program look and perform like the other, but it doesn't change the basic nature of either program. Satan is the great emulator. He has sinners who act more saintly than saints even though they are on their way to hell, and he likes to see saints who act more sinful than sinners even though they are on their way to heaven.

The identity of both groups remains the same, but they have plugged into an emulator so they think they're the opposite of what they actually are, and they act that way. They've been deceived, and so they live in their deception as if it were the real deal when it is not.

THE DECEIVER'S METHOD

As we suggested above, the method Satan uses to work his deception is to get to our minds.

His concern is not a person's circumstances. Whether you're poor, middle class, or rich doesn't matter to him, because if he gets your mind he has everything.

Messing with Your Mind

When I say Satan likes to mess with your mind, I'm talking about your thoughts. What he does is plant his thoughts in your mind until his thoughts become your thoughts. Satan repeats them over and over until you begin to believe they are your thoughts.

When Satan said to Eve, "You will be like God," whose thought was that? Eve didn't come up with it. That came from the mouth of the one who said, "I will make myself like the Most High" (Isaiah 14:14).

That was Satan's thought, but he planted it in Eve's mind until she began to think all of this was her idea. You can see the shift in thinking in Genesis 3:6, when Eve looked at the tree and began to desire it. It took the serpent five verses to think his thoughts in Eve's mind. But by the time we get to verse 6, his thoughts have become her thoughts.

When a believer says, "I can't make this marriage work," whose thought is that? "I can't get rid of this habit." Really? Who told you that? "I'm a nobody. I'm nothing, and I always will be nothing." Who's doing the talking here?

Satan has been programming his thoughts into the minds of many Christians for so long they can't tell the difference anymore. The old serpent is crafty. He wraps himself around a person's mind, and then like a python he puts the squeeze on until that person can't break the serpent's hold.

The devil has been at this deception for a long time. He got to King David's mind one day. "Then Satan stood up against Israel and moved David to number Israel" (1 Chronicles 21:1). Satan told David, "Count your people to see how strong you are."

But David thought it was his own idea, so he said, "I think I'll take a census of the people." That was a sinful action because it demonstrated reliance on human strength rather than God, and God judged Israel severely for David's sin.

The Bible says Satan also "put [it] into the heart" of Judas to betray Jesus (John 13:2). Peter said to Ananias, "Why has Satan filled your heart to lie to the Holy Spirit?" (Acts 5:3).

Satan convinced Ananias and his wife, Sapphira, to hold back some of the money they got for selling a piece of land and to pretend that they were giving the full amount to the church in Jerusalem. We can imagine the conversation these two had as they discussed what they thought was their plan, which cost them their lives.

The devil even convinced Peter that it was a good idea to try to keep Jesus from going to the cross. When Jesus announced He was going to be crucified, Peter blurted out, "God forbid it, Lord! This shall never happen to You" (Matthew 16:22).

But Jesus stunned Peter by telling him, "Get behind Me, Satan!" (v. 23). The words were Peter's, but the thoughts came from Satan. When the devil gets our minds, we start thinking his thoughts without even being aware that he's in the vicinity.

Capturing Your Emotions

Once Satan gets your mind, he will transfer those thoughts to your emotions. Our thoughts don't simply stay on the intellectual level, because we are emotional beings. We begin to feel what we think.

The devil wants to capture our emotions because feelings are so dominating. Most people live and make decisions by their feelings. There's nothing wrong with our emotions, but they can lead us in the wrong direction.

"I don't feel love for my wife anymore." "I've lost all feelings for my husband." Emotions are very real, even when they're wrong. After Satan gets us to think his thoughts, he wants us to *feel* that these thoughts are right.

Guiding Your Actions

This is the next logical step in the deceiver's method. Along with our minds and emotions come our hands and feet—our actions.

The process is so clear in the case of Eve. Once the serpent got Eve thinking that being like God was a pretty good idea, the Bible says she *desired* the fruit of the forbidden tree. Now Eve's emotions were being stirred. She was getting excited about the idea of being as wise as God. So with her thoughts in gear and her emotions engaged, she reached out for the fruit and acted on her wrong thinking and wrong emotions. Adam joined her in buying Satan's lie, although Adam wasn't directly deceived (1 Timothy 2:14), and the human race was plunged into sin.

Jesus called Satan "the father of lies" (John 8:44). Fathers produce children who bear their image, so Satan's job is to produce lies that look and sound just like him. Anytime a lie is conceived and born, Satan is behind the process. So when we start believing that his thoughts are our thoughts, we are believing lies.

THE RESULT OF SATAN'S DECEPTION

Once Eve disobeyed God and Adam followed, the rest of Genesis 3 explains all that they lost as a result of Satan's deception. These losses are important to understand because the human race is still suffering from them.

Before Satan entered the picture, Adam and Eve had everything, all of it given to them by God. Adam didn't have to break into a sweat, because God gave him the perfect job. He didn't have to go looking for a wife; God *made* him a wife. The two didn't even have to struggle over their spiritual life, because they had perfect fellowship with God.

But after our first parents became self-sufficient and decided they didn't need God anymore, look how much they lost.

A String of Devastating Losses

The biggest loss Adam and Eve suffered was spiritual—the loss of intimacy and communication with God. They died spiritually the moment they disobeyed God, and according to Genesis 3:8 they hid from God's presence for the first time. Instead of running to God, they were running from God. Every person since then has been born spiritually dead.

Adam and Eve also suffered a devastating physical loss. The curse God pronounced on each of them involved pain, sweat, and hard labor. And of course both of them eventually died. Sickness and death, as well as economic hardships, became their portion because they had rebelled against God.

Fear was another result of Satan's deception. Adam and Eve hid from God because, according to Adam, "I was afraid" (Genesis 3:10). In other words, their emotions were messed up. They had never been afraid before. Are you living in fear today? You need to know that the root of fear is the desire to be self-sufficient and independent from God. When Adam was in right relationship with God, he was secure. But when that intimacy was lost, fear replaced security.

Here's another big loss. Adam and Eve were messed up relationally because from then on men and women would be engaged in a "battle of the sexes." The story of man-woman relationships under the curse of sin is a story of the struggle for control and independence. Married couples don't get along because of "personality differences." That originated in the Garden.

Given all of this, it's not surprising that Satan's deception of our first parents also led to the loss of their psychological wholeness.

Satan robbed the human race blind when he tempted Adam and Eve in Eden.

A lot of Christians get nervous when someone mentions psychology. But psychology is simply a study of the soul. It comes from the Greek word *psyche,* which means "soul." Your soul is made up of three parts: your intellect, the ability to think; your will, the ability to choose; and your emotions, the ability to feel. It's your personality.

Psychology is a valid discipline when it is rooted in good theology. Psychology that is rooted in a biblical view of mankind can analyze the soul and help us understand why we are the way we are and why we do the things we do.

It's one thing to identify a problem, but it's another thing altogether to tell a person how to fix it. That's where the problem usually comes in. Psychotherapy, for example, is often rooted in a non-Christian view of the human personality. So the patient gets treatment that totally ignores his spiritual makeup and leaves him more messed up than when he started.

When God created Adam, He breathed life into him and Adam became "a living being," which literally means "a living soul" (Genesis 2:7). This gave Adam the capacity for fellowship with God, which was destroyed by sin. Any analysis of human nature that doesn't take this into account is bound to lead to mistaken conclusions.

Robbed of God's Gifts

To borrow a common expression, Satan robbed the human race blind when he tempted Adam and Eve in Eden. Jesus described Satan as a thief whose only purpose is "to steal and kill and destroy" (John 10:10).

Satan is still doing his thing, robbing God's people of the gifts He wants us to have, including our joy, peace, and purpose. Are you ever stumped about what to do or where to go next? That confusion is the result of Satan's work. Before their fall, the only wrong choice Scripture tells us that Adam and Eve could make was to eat the forbidden fruit. Every other option they had was a good one. But after they sinned, they had all kinds of good and bad choices to make.

The devil is also stealing our financial blessings by tying us up in debt that's often the result of a greedy desire for more. We get those letters congratulating us on our outstanding credit and offering us another shiny card that will give us the buying power and financial independence we so richly deserve. But the back end of that deal is financial bondage that could take us years to get out of.

Even more tragically than all of this, the devil is stealing our marriages and our families. We're told that divorce among Christians has now caught up with, and is surpassing, the national average. I'll have a lot more to say about this area. One reason Satan is so successful is that he never tells you the real deal up front. If a thief with a gun and a mask knocked on your front door and asked to come in, what would you do? You'd slam the door and lock it and call 911 right away.

But thieves don't do that. They're deceptive, sneaking into the house when no one is looking. Since Satan is a master deceiver, we need to be on the alert for his approach.

OUR RESPONSE TO SATAN'S DECEPTION

How should we respond to Satan's deception? Becoming more aware of his wiles and being on guard against them is a good place to start.

But more than that, I'm convinced that Christians will never be truly free until we understand who we are in Christ and start living like who we really are. We need to get our identity back.

Someone may be saying, "Tony, that sounds great. But what about the problem I'm already in? How do I begin getting free from the chains that are holding me in bondage?"

Good question. Let me answer it this way. In the 1800s, many Asians were brought to America as indentured servants. Their hope was to work and earn enough to eventually buy their way out of servitude.

But there was a problem. The people who employed these Asian immigrants didn't pay them enough to keep up with what it cost them to live, let alone to save any money toward purchasing their freedom.

You don't have to be an accountant to know that if you're making less money than it costs you to live, you aren't going to make any progress. The overseers of these indentured servants paid them just enough to keep them in perpetual bondage.

A person in that situation only has one hope for freedom. Someone else is going to have to pay the bill to set him or her free. Jesus Christ did that for us when He died on the cross to forgive us of our sins.

If you aren't sure of your relationship to Christ, you need to be set free from your sins, because you can never work your way into being right with God. This is accomplished by placing your faith in Christ alone as your Sin-Bearer.

But the freedom Christ purchased for us goes further than our salvation. Not only is it impossible to work your way to heaven by your own efforts, but it's impossible for you to work your way out of spiritual bondage by self-effort. That's why so many Christians are not enjoying their freedom. They're like Adam and Eve, saying to God, "I can do this myself."

Too many of us are like hamsters on treadmills in their cages. We can see freedom and we want freedom, but after spending endless hours running faster and faster on our spiritual treadmills, all we manage to do is exhaust ourselves. True freedom for a hamster only comes when its owner reaches down and lifts it out of its cage, while still keeping the hamster in the owner's protective care.

The route to spiritual freedom as a Christian is the same route you took to become a Christian: complete dependence on Christ. As you read on in this book, ask Him to show you your true identity as a believer, and then ask Him to empower you to live out that identity by the Holy Spirit's power.

Chapter Two

CLARIFYING YOUR IDENTITY

If you were to ask people, "Who is Michael Jordan?" most would probably say he was a great basketball player.

Jordan *was* great—probably the greatest basketball player ever to play the game. But is that the right or wrong answer concerning who Michael Jordan is? It's wrong. Why? Because being a basketball player does not tell us who Jordan *is*, just what he used to do.

Do you see my point? If the totality of Michael Jordan's identity was wrapped up in his being a professional athlete, what is he now that he's retired—a nonperson? Did Jordan cease to exist the day he retired from basketball? Of course not.

That's why one of the greatest mistakes you can make is to define yourself by what you do for a living. And yet that's the primary yardstick people, especially men, use to measure each other. Let two men meet, and the first thing they want to know is, "What do you do for a living?" And if a man has a big job with a prestigious title, he must be somebody.

In fact, some people go to great lengths to get the right identity.

They'll pay plastic surgeons to change their appearance in order to look like someone they're not. They'll seek better-paying jobs to enhance their status and seek friends who will help them look good. Some people will even buy diplomas and degrees from mail-order houses so they can appear impressive.

But if your identity as a person is rooted in your performance, you will always misdefine yourself—even if you're considered successful. This issue has an important spiritual component, because Satan knows that if he can keep you from discovering your true identity as a Christian, he can hold you hostage. He can block your spiritual inheritance and keep you from enjoying victory, because you can't be liberated if you don't know who you are.

That's why for us as Christians, knowing our true spiritual identity is the master key to unlock the door of victory in every area of life. We must know who we are. To understand that, we need to turn to God's Word, because you and I are who God says we are, not who Satan says we are.

Let's begin clarifying your identity.

THE KEY TO YOUR IDENTITY

First of all, I want to talk about the key to your identity. The principle here is that your identity is always and only linked to your birth.

Peter wrote, "Blessed be the God and Father of our Lord Jesus Christ, who according to His great mercy has caused us to be born again to a living hope through the resurrection of Jesus Christ from the dead." Then he adds, "You have been born again not of seed which is perishable but imperishable, that is, through the living and enduring word of God" (1 Peter 1:3, 23).

Your Birth Sets Your Destiny

Peter was writing about the new birth, by which a person dies to the old life of sin and is born again through faith in Christ. It is our new birth as Christians that gives us hope and determines our eternal destiny. Notice that Peter didn't say anything about what we do for a living, much less what non-Christians can do to make themselves acceptable to God.

This is so fundamental because it explains why even the best non-Christians are unacceptable to God. We all know people who don't know the Lord but who are friendly and helpful and all of that—the kind of people you want to live or work next to.

But the Bible says these people are not acceptable to God because they have a "birth" defect. All of us are born with the inherited sin of Adam attached to us. We are born in a lost condition, cut off from God and under His judgment. We have a birth defect that can never be solved by our performance, no matter how kind or loving or charitable we are.

What we need is to be born again. Not "good again" or "better again," but a new birth that radically changes our identity and places us in the family of God. Identity is determined by birth, and when it comes to our eternal destiny, God relates to us based on our new birth or lack thereof. Jesus told Nicodemus he would not see the kingdom of God unless he was "born again" (John 3:3, cf. v. 5).

Birth determines identity on the human level too. I'm an Evans by birth, and I will always be the son of Arthur and Evelyn Evans, even if I were to embarrass the Evans name.

The same goes for my children. They are who they are because they were born into our family, not because they performed their way into our family. They don't have to struggle or work hard to be Evanses. Their birth settled the issue of their identity, and we have birth certificates to prove their identity.

We know that we don't have to work to be someone we already are, and yet we have Christians who are working hard to be Christians. They say, "Well, you know, I'm trying to live like a Christian." Wrong! Trying has nothing to do with being a Christian. You are either born again and a Christian by virtue of that birth, or you are a non-Christian still in your sins.

Determining Identity by Performance

Remember our opening illustration about Michael Jordan? We said that the problem of tying Jordan's identity to his basketball career is that he doesn't play anymore. But he's still a person made in God's image and of infinite value to God, just as you and I are.

In fact, the problem with some pro athletes is that, as far as they're concerned, their identity *is* tied to their careers. This is why so many ex-athletes struggle to adjust to life after their playing days are over. They don't know what to do or where to go because they've lost their identity.

But sports stars aren't the only people who run into trouble when they try to attach their identity to what they do. Take the case of a person who says, "I'm a Christian. I've accepted Christ as my Savior and been born again, but I use illegal drugs. I've tried to quit many times, but I always fall back into the habit. I guess I'm just a drug addict."

It's possible that a person like this isn't really a Christian at all. But for the sake of the illustration, let's say he is a genuine Christian, a true child of God. If that's the case, this person is identifying himself as a drug addict because he is doing the things addicts do. He has confused his performance with his identity. He has convinced himself, "I do what drug addicts do, so I must be a drug addict." No, he is a Christian with a serious drug problem.

Identity is determined by birth.

You could also substitute other sins into this formula, such as homosexuality. The world wants us to believe that people are homosexual by birth, not by choice. But a homosexual who believes that has badly confused identity with performance. That's what Satan wants, because he knows we will function based on our perception of ourselves.

Once he gets us thinking we are someone we're not, he's got us. Nobody is born a drug addict or a homosexual. Christians may be performing in these unacceptable ways, but that's not who they are. It's an identity issue.

Don't misunderstand. Just because we are not to identify ourselves by our actions doesn't mean we can deny or excuse our wrong actions. Make no mistake, a Christian who is battling the sins we mentioned above, or any other problem, needs to confess it and deal with it and turn from it, no matter what it takes.

But the principle still stands. Identity is determined by birth. When I think of this, I think of a young man named Ikki Soma who used to serve as my pastoral intern at our church in Dallas.

Ikki is Japanese by birth, but he grew up black. His college roommate was black. He was the only Japanese member of an otherwise all-black track team in college. His seminary roommate was black. His favorite music is hip-hop and soul. His favorite meal is fried catfish with hot sauce, macaroni and cheese, mustard greens, corn bread, and iced tea.

When Ikki preaches, he preaches black. And he is married to a wonderful black Christian woman. Everything about Ikki's external world is black.

But when Ikki fills out an official form that asks for his race, guess what race he marks? Not black, even though his "performance" is black. Ikki marks Japanese because that's what he is by birth. Again, it is birth, not performance, that determines identity.

THE ESSENCE OF YOUR IDENTITY

Here are two verses that help to explain the essence of your identity as a Christian.

Peter wrote, "[God] has granted to us His precious and magnificent promises, so that by them you may become partakers of the divine nature, having escaped the corruption that is in the world by lust" (2 Peter 1:4).

The apostle Paul described salvation this way: "If anyone is in Christ, he is a new creature; the old things passed away; behold, new things have come" (2 Corinthians 5:17).

Your New Nature in Christ

When you were born again, God deposited within you a new nature that wasn't there before, a nature that is now the core of who you are. Peter called it "the divine nature" because it is the very life of God.

So if you have trusted Jesus Christ for eternal life, the very life of God is the core of your new reality. God placed His essence, which is spirit, at the center of your being.

That's why if you are in Christ, you are brand-new. You are not the same person you were before, even though you may be doing things you did before. Why is that? Because your identity is in your birth.

Changing Your Actions

Do you get the message? We are new people in Christ. The old life is gone. But if this is true, why are so many believers controlled by their old ways and old habits? Because Satan has fed them the lie that they're the same old people they used to be. And we act in accordance with the way we perceive ourselves.

As I studied the material for this book, it dawned on me that too many times we go about it the wrong way in trying to get Christians to straighten their lives up. We spend all of our time telling believers to stop doing wrong things and start doing right things.

But the problem isn't simply that Christians do wrong things and need to be told to do right things. The problem is that they're confused about who they are. They are experiencing a major identity crisis. And as we've seen, once you become confused about your identity, you won't know what to stop doing and what to start doing. Changing our actions starts with clarifying our identity.

It's possible to get people to conform on the outside without this inner change. But it won't last. Some people still want to follow their old ways; they just don't want anyone to know how carnal they are. So they sin in private and wear a mask of spirituality in public.

The story is told that the queen of England was trying to get her daughter to sit still. She started the way most parents start. "Young lady, be still." That worked for a while, but the girl started wiggling again. Then it was, "I said, be still!"

But nothing worked to keep the girl quiet until the queen said, "Young lady, be still. Don't you know who you are?" In other words, "You're a princess. Act like it." The girl got the message this time, because the queen tied her daughter's behavior to her identity.

We can tell each other all day to stop doing this or that. But if we don't see the connection between our identity in Christ and our actions, I'm going to start wiggling after a while, and so will you.

Don't Hang Out at the Cemetery

We read earlier that our old life "passed away" when we came to Christ. We are no longer the people we were before we became Christians. When somebody passes away, we hold a funeral and say good-bye to that person. Living according to our old identity is like hanging out at the cemetery long after the funeral is over.

I know the question that a lot of believers raise at this point: If our old life has passed away, why do we still want to do the same old things? That's a crucial issue we'll deal with in a future chapter.

Just let me remind you that we still live in bodies that are corrupted by sin. As long as we are on earth, we will carry the principle of sin dwelling within us. The Bible says there is nothing good in our "flesh," the old life, which we will struggle against until we get to heaven (Romans 7:18–20). But we have every means necessary for victory.

My purpose in this chapter is to help you grasp the reality of your new identity, because once you know who you are in Christ, nothing can stop you from living right—and wanting to do it. And by the way, the divine nature within you is perfect. It cannot practice sin as a way of life, because it is "born of God" (1 John 3:9).

So when we say, "I'm only human," that's not true anymore. Satan knows it, but he wants to keep us from knowing it so he can keep the handcuffs on us.

THE DESIGNATION OF YOUR NEW IDENTITY

So if we're not the people we used to be, who are we? What is our biblical designation? The Bible uses a lot of descriptive terms and titles for Christians. I want to look at one of those terms and then at one of the most important titles God uses for us.

A "Living Dead Person"

Galatians 2:20 contains a key principle for understanding our spiritual identity. This great verse, which is my life verse, says, "I have been crucified with Christ; and it is no longer I who live, but Christ lives in me; and the life which I now live in the flesh I live by faith in the Son of God, who loved me, and delivered Himself up for me."

According to Paul, you're a dead person. Nevertheless, you're a living dead person because you are alive through Jesus Christ, who lives within you. We could say you are a "dead man walking." Galatians 2:20 is a core verse for the concepts I'll be talking about throughout this book, and I'll be referring to it more than once.

Crucifixion means death. Whatever we were before we came to Christ died with Him on the cross and was buried when He was buried. For this reason, I no longer buy the popular saying that Christians are just "sinners saved by grace." It would be more accurate to say we *were* sinners before we were saved by grace. God has a different designation for us now.

Saints, Not Sinners

Here's a one-question Bible quiz: What was the most carnal, sin-riddled church in the New Testament? Answer: Corinth. This was the most messed-up group of Christians you could imagine. They not only tolerated an incestuous situation, but they bragged about it (1 Corinthians 5:1–2).

And when these folk came to church, they would sit on opposite sides because they were mad at each other (1 Corinthians 11:18–19). Now there's a problem we don't have in the church anymore, right? As the teenagers would say, "Yeah, right!"

The Corinthians were also stuffing themselves and getting drunk at church during the meal that accompanied the Lord's Supper (11:20–21). Paul even said some of them had died as a result of God's discipline (v. 30). First Corinthians 13, the great chapter on love that we get all teary-eyed over, was actually a stinging rebuke to this church's lack of love.

You get the idea. Paul had very little to commend the Corinthians for in his first letter, but before he got down to all the spiritual dirt, he addressed them as "saints by calling" (1 Corinthians 1:2).

The word *saint* means a "set-apart one." It speaks of our relationship to Christ. We belong to Him now. This is our new identity. Paul's message to the Corinthians was one we're becoming familiar with: "You're not the same people you used to be before you got saved, even though you're doing a lot of the same things you used to do before you got saved. God now calls you saints."

Believers are called saints sixty times in the New Testament. We may be carnal saints, defeated saints, and even sinning saints. But we're still God's "set-apart ones."

That name gives us great hope for changing our actions. Once we understand that we are saints, we can work with that. You are not just a patched-up, converted sinner. You are holy in God's sight.

I like the analogy of caterpillars and butterflies. When was the last time you heard someone call a butterfly a "converted caterpillar"? It was a caterpillar, but it has taken on a whole new character and a new name. It may be a wounded, broken, and defeated butterfly—but a butterfly it is.

Before you met Christ, you were a spiritual caterpillar. You may have been a good-looking and well-connected caterpillar—but a caterpillar you were. However, when you put your faith in Jesus Christ, you became a butterfly. You are called a saint.

THE DIFFERENCE YOUR NEW IDENTITY MAKES

Let's get practical as we close out this chapter by answering the question, "So what? What difference does it make that I'm a saint?"

We hinted at this difference earlier, but let me spell it out again. If you know Jesus Christ and you're struggling with homosexual desires, you are not a homosexual. You are a saint whom Satan wants to dupe into believing that you are trapped in this behavior because this is the way God made you.

The difference is that knowing your true identity gives you hope for change. There's nothing more hopeless than being told you have no way out of your problem.

But as I said earlier, the truth of our identity in Christ also means we have to do something about our wrong actions. Let me give you a real-life illustration of the problems we get into when we act according to our flesh, and then talk about how to come out against the devil and for Christ.

Using the Old Reference Point

One of the best illustrations of this problem is one I see all the time in my pastoral ministry. It occurs with married people who still want to think and act as if they're single.

Most people understand that when they get married, they are surrendering their singleness. If you're married, what you did as a single person is largely irrelevant now. Unfortunately, some married people don't see why a little thing like a wedding should interfere with their lifestyle.

Some married men still want to hang out with the guys and come in when they feel like it, just like they did before they got married. To them, getting married means little more than adding a wife to their list of hobbies and interests.

Our society encourages this kind of schizophrenic thinking about marriage by encouraging couples to pursue their own separate careers and lives. In this setup, the marriage is more of a business arrangement or a convenience than a covenantal, lifelong commitment.

When these people say, "I'm the same person I was before I got married," they mean that literally. I'm not saying husbands and wives can't pursue their careers. I'm talking about a worldview that says, "I will to attach myself to you, but at the core of my being I'm still going to function as if I'm single."

Now I realize it takes time to get used to a new identity. After my daughter Priscilla had been married for about a month, she came to me one day asking for money. I had two words for her: "Ask Jerry."

You see, Priscilla is now the wife of Jerry Shirer. Things are different now. Of course, she's still my daughter and an Evans by birth. But her primary identity is now found in her relationship to her husband, not to her mother and me. Priscilla had to get used to that new reference point, and so did I.

Let me tell you something. Satan needs to get used to the fact that you don't belong to him anymore! He needs to understand that things are different now. You have a new name and a new relationship. You don't live where you used to live anymore. The sin that used to tie you up doesn't have any power over you any longer. That's not who you are.

Coming Out Against Satan

I'm sure you're familiar with the federal witness protection program. If a government case has a key witness whose life may be in danger, they keep that witness under wraps and hidden away before the trial.

But once the witness takes the stand and testifies against the Mafia kingpin or whoever is on trial, everyone in the courtroom knows who he is. So the government takes elaborate steps to protect that person.

The basic objective of the witness protection program is very simple. It is designed to give the endangered person a new identity. He and his family are relocated and given new names. Their old identities are, for all practical purposes, erased from the record as if they never existed. All of this is done so the enemy can't make any claim on the life of that witness who has come out and testified against him.

It's time for a lot of Christians to stand up and testify against the devil. My prayer is that when the truth of your new identity gets down into your soul, you are going to come out against the Enemy. You are going to step into the courtroom of heaven and say, "I am no longer under Satan's authority. I've been made new by the blood of Christ. The devil isn't going to intimidate me anymore."

When you come out against him, the devil isn't going to like it. But God has a wonderful "witness protection program." He has set you up with a brand-new identity. The old records have been erased, which means they aren't there for Satan to use against you. He can't locate you anymore, because you don't live where you used to live. Are you ready to enter God's witness protection program? It's good for all eternity!

Chapter Three

YOUR NEW POSITION IN CHRIST

Commuters in large cities like Dallas are used to hearing rush-hour traffic reports on the radio. Those reports used to come exclusively from a reporter in a helicopter high over the freeways. But with cell phones so common, at least one of our local stations now encourages its listeners to call in if they spot a traffic problem. Of course, the callers are usually already stuck in the middle of the mess by the time they call, so they can't tell other drivers what alternate routes to take to avoid the problem, how long the backup is, or whether the accident or whatever is causing the problem has been cleared away.

I don't know about you, but if I'm trying to get to work in the morning and there's trouble ahead on the freeway, I want help from someone who can see the whole picture and tell me what to do. I want to get my traffic reports from the helicopter, from someone who is in an elevated position surveying the entire scene. When I need perspective on a traffic snarl, I don't necessarily want to hear from someone at ground level who is too deeply immersed in the problem to see above or around it.

It strikes me that too many Christians are like drivers in a traffic jam, trying to get perspective while stuck in the middle of the problem. The Christian life was never meant to be lived from a limited, ground-level position. If we want to live as victorious, liberated Christians, we need to elevate our position so that we rise above ground level and see the big picture.

Satan wants to keep you stuck in traffic, but God wants to "helicopter" you above that mess and give you a view of life from the top. In fact, God has already done that, the day you trusted Christ as your Savior. You not only received a new life and a new identity, you were elevated to a new position in Christ.

THE PRINCIPLE OF YOUR NEW POSITION

When we talk about a Christian's new spiritual position, we are referring to the way God views us in Christ—and, therefore, the way we should view ourselves.

This last part is critical, because we are now totally identified with Christ. God doesn't see you the way He saw you before you were a Christian.

The Way Things Are

One reason this truth is so important is that this is not simply a theory of how things could be or ought to be. Your new position in Christ is a present reality, a statement of how things actually are as far as God is concerned. This principle is transforming when it is understood and applied.

The Bible tells us, "In Him [Christ] all the fullness of Deity dwells in bodily form, and in Him you have been made complete, and He is the head over all rule and authority" (Colossians 2:9–10).

Since all the fullness of God—total deity—dwells in Christ, and Christ is in you (see Colossians 1:27), what also dwells in you? The fullness of God. Certainly not in the absolute sense that is true of Christ, because He *is* God. But if God is living in you through Christ, what else do you need? Nothing. That's why Paul said believers are complete in Christ. Colossions 2:12 goes on to explain that God did this by reclassifying and reidentifying you with the death and resurrection of Jesus.

Enveloped in God

When I taught this principle at our church, I brought with me three envelopes of different sizes and a slip of paper. It was a basic illustration that I think will be helpful here.

The slip of paper had "Jesus" written on it. The smallest of the three envelopes had my name on it, the middle-sized envelope was labeled "Jesus," and the largest envelope was labeled "God," meaning God the Father.

The Bible says that when I accepted Christ, He came to live within me. So I put the slip of paper representing Jesus inside the envelope with my name on it, to illustrate the fact that Christ indwells me.

But it doesn't stop there. In John 14:20, Jesus told His disciples, "In that day you will know that I am in My Father, and you in Me, and I in you." That's the same principle Paul was teaching in Colossians 2.

So not only is Christ in me, but I am also in Christ. I took the small envelope representing me, with Jesus on the inside, and slipped it in the next larger envelope, which again stood for Christ. But because Christ is also in God, I took the whole thing and put it inside the largest envelope.

Now here's the beauty of this truth. How can anyone, Satan included, get to Tony Evans? First, he has to go through God the Father. Even if that were possible, what would you find if you tore open the envelope representing God? You'd find the envelope with Christ's name on it. So to get to Tony Evans, he has to go through Christ too.

For the sake of the illustration, let's suppose the devil opened the envelope marked "Jesus" and took out the one with my name on it. Would he have me then? No, because when you open up Tony Evans, you find out he has Jesus inside of him!

I encourage you to do this exercise for yourself. It's a good visual aid to drive home the reality of your new position in Christ—a truth Satan doesn't want you to understand because it will help expose him as the toothless lion he is.

Christ changed your identity from sinner to saint, and He repositioned you so that you are now completely enveloped in Him. He has also relocated you from earth to heaven.

THE PLACE OF YOUR NEW POSITION

I love Ephesians 2, the passage that is the Magna Carta of our exalted position in Jesus Christ. The chapter opens with you and me "dead in [o]ur trespasses and sins" (vv. 1–3)—stopped dead in the middle of a spiritual traffic jam, if you will.

"Helicoptered Out"

But then God came down in His grace and "helicoptered" us out by sending Jesus Christ to die for our sins. Not only that, but we were lifted to the highest position possible.

Paul described the process this way: We were dead in sins, "but God, being rich in mercy, because of His great love with which He loved us, even when we were dead in our transgressions, made us alive together with Christ (by grace you have been saved), and raised us up with Him, and seated us with Him in the heavenly places in Christ Jesus" (Ephesians 2:4–6).

We became so intimately linked with Christ in salvation that when God raised Jesus from the dead and seated His Son "at His right hand in the heavenly places" (Ephesians 1:20), we came along too! Where Jesus is, we are. When God looks to His right and sees Jesus, He sees us sitting there with Him.

That's spiritual reality, not make-believe. Compare Ephesians 1:20 with 2:6, and you'll see something interesting. God raised Jesus up and seated Him—past tense. God raised us up and seated us—past tense. They're the same two verbs, except that the verbs in 2:6 have a prefix that means "with."

This means that what happened to Jesus two thousand years ago became your experience when you accepted Christ. So now when God wants to relate to you and work with you, He does so based upon your new position. Your physical frame may be in an easy chair in your living room right now as you read this book. But as a believer that is not your primary location.

This teaching can be difficult to grasp, I know, because sometimes it's hard for us to see beyond the world around us. Maybe it will help you to compare it to teleconferencing in business.

Thanks to this technology, a person can sit in Dallas and still attend a meeting taking place in the company's boardroom in Chicago. The teleconference connects everyone involved by video screens, so the person in Dallas can fully interact with everyone in Chicago and discuss decisions or whatever else is needed.

The person in Dallas is as much a part of the meeting as the people in Chicago. And you can be sure that if this person is an executive in that company, any orders he or she gives will be duly noted and carried out. No one will be able to say, "Well, I didn't think I needed to take you seriously because, after all, you weren't physically there in the room with us."

The Bible says that God has "teleconferenced" you to heaven, right into the boardroom. You are there right now, seated next to Jesus Christ. Of course, there is a sense in which we will not be fully in heaven until we go there and receive our new bodies, but that doesn't lessen the spiritual reality of this one bit.

Struggling to Breathe

Whenever you change your position, by necessity you change your perspective. When you look at life from the elevated vantage point of your position in the heavenly places with Christ, things that look chaotic and out of order on earth suddenly take orderly shape, the way fields and houses do when we look at them from an airplane. God is saying that if we want to be free, we need to start living life from our new vantage point.

Let me change the imagery to show you the difference that your new position makes. Scuba divers are able to go down into the sea, even though water is an alien environment for humans. But the only way divers can function down there is by bringing their life from above down with them in the form of their air tanks.

Scuba divers may look like fish with their fins and all, but they're aliens whose real life is found above the water. Take away the divers' oxygen tanks and they'll start gasping for air and having all kinds of serious problems.

Believers are aliens in a foreign environment here on earth. Our life, our breath, is from above, where we are seated with Christ. Take away our position in Christ and we will begin to gasp for spiritual oxygen.

So guess who's trying to cut off your supply of spiritual oxygen? Satan wants you to dive into the water without your life-giving supply of oxygen from God, so you'll run out of breath trying to live the Christian life.

The problem is that too many of us are trying to breathe underwater on our own, and we aren't made for that. So let's get our heads above water and take a deep, rejuvenating breath of the pure oxygen of our exalted position in Christ.

THE POWER OF YOUR NEW POSITION

Did you know that there is also a new spiritual power that comes with your new position? When you linked up with Jesus Christ, you were joined to the most powerful force in the universe.

The Bible says that when God raised Jesus from the dead and seated Him at His right hand, Jesus assumed a place of power "far above all rule and authority and power and dominion, and every name that is named, not only in this age but also in the one to come" (Ephesians 1:21).

Nothing is exempted from Jesus' dominion, and that includes Satan. Jesus has already taken care of the devil.

The Bible says that Christ disarmed Satan when He died on the cross and rose again (Colossians 2:14–15). According to the writer of Hebrews, Jesus died so that "through death He might render powerless him who had the power of death, that is, the devil" (2:14). Paul wrote, "The God of peace will soon crush Satan under your feet" (Romans 16:20).

Jesus has conquered Satan. So if you're seated with Jesus, guess where you sit today in relation to the devil? You're sitting far above him.

Someone may be asking, "If Jesus Christ has all this power and I'm seated with Him, why am I not experiencing this power in my life?" Because Satan has kept many of us from realizing our position and living accordingly, regularly drawing on the spiritual power available to us.

The Enemy can't get to Jesus because He is seated far too high for the Enemy to reach. We aren't exempt from Satan's attacks the way Jesus is. But when it comes to pulling us down from our lofty position, Satan can't really get to us unless we let him. There is safety in the heavenly places, and power too. We need to go up high where God is located so the Enemy can't get to us.

THE PRACTICALITY OF YOUR NEW POSITION

We'll take the rest of the chapter on this final point, since so many Christians need help taking the truth of their exalted position from theory to practice.

The good news is that this isn't some hidden truth just for theologians and preachers. Three simple, very practical words from the book of Romans will help you grab hold of this concept and fix it in your mind and heart.

The Bible says that when it comes to your position as a believer, there is something you need to *know,* to *consider,* and to *present.* These three words will transport you to the boardroom in heavenly places. Let's take them one at a time.

What You Need to Know

First, there is a vital principle you need to know because it is true and already at work within you: You must understand that when you accepted Jesus Christ as your Savior and became a new creation in Him, your sin nature was put to death. Christ has destroyed the power of sin in your life. The old you died at the cross.

Why do you need to know this? Because you won't always feel it. In fact, you may already be questioning the idea that your sin nature no longer exists. A lot of Christians want to know, "If my sin nature is dead, why am I having so much trouble with it? Why is sin kicking the living daylights out of me?"

We'll deal with this in the next chapter, so I don't want to get too deeply into it now. It is true that the experience of many believers doesn't match what God's Word says about their sin nature.

Let me just say here that the reason we sin as believers is not because we still have a sin nature. It's because our new nature resides in a body so contaminated by sin that it doesn't know how to do anything else.

This is why your old body is going to become worm food someday when you die. But until then, you and I will still battle the problem of indwelling sin. This is the war within that's our subject in the next chapter.

Only the power of Jesus Christ can shut down the sin factory.

With that background, let's go to Scripture and see the truth that our sin nature was put to death in Christ. Paul wove this principle throughout his teaching in Romans 6, so we need to pick up several phrases and verses.

"Do you not know that all of us who have been baptized into Christ Jesus have been baptized into His death? Therefore we have been buried with Him through baptism into death" (vv. 3–4a). When Christ died, we died too.

Paul continued by saying, "We have become united with Him in the likeness of His death" (v. 5). Then comes this crucial statement: "Knowing this, that our old self was crucified with Him, in order that our body of sin might be done away with, so that we would no longer be slaves to sin" (v. 6).

Paul asked, "Do you not know?" and then he answered the question of what we need to know. The reality is that when our old self was crucified with Christ, our "sin factory" was shut down. That's what the sin nature is, a factory constantly turning out sin the way a car factory turns out cars.

That's why non-Christians cannot ultimately solve their problem of sin. Even though they may fix one or two sins, the factory is still in business. Only the power of Jesus Christ can shut down the sin factory.

Now as I said, we still sin as Christians. We'll see later that Paul wrestled with this too. Sometimes he didn't do what he really wanted to do, and he did the very thing he didn't want to do. His conclusion? "I am no longer the one doing it, but sin which dwells in me" (Romans 7:20).

That's the issue we referred to above, the principle of indwelling sin that has lodged in our old bodies. But don't miss what the Bible is saying. We don't have the factory anymore. We are new creations in Christ; the old has gone (see 2 Corinthians 5:17).

You see, this is a different problem than having a sin nature producing sin. The problem of indwelling sin is one we can handle. If God wants you to know this, you can be sure Satan *doesn't* want you to know it.

Why? Because once you find out your sin factory has been condemned and closed, you just might start acting like it. You might start singing and rejoicing, the way the people did in the *Wizard of* Oz when Dorothy's house fell on the wicked witch and she was no more.

We need to start praising God that the "wicked witch" is dead! When you sin as a child of God, it's not the real you sinning because your sin nature is dead. It's still possible for you to sin because you are living in a sin-contaminated body, and you're still responsible for your sin. But sin is no longer the ruling principle of your life. That's a truth we can work with.

Before we were saved, we were so accustomed to sin that it wore a groove into our hearts and minds, like a river cutting a gorge through rock. What we need to do is make some new grooves. That's why the Bible says we have to be transformed by the renewing of our minds (see Romans 12:1–2).

What You Need to Consider

Knowing is important, but there's more to the process. The second of the three words that help us get a handle on our position is found in Romans 6:11. "Even so consider yourselves to be dead to sin, but alive to God in Christ Jesus."

To consider means to count it to be true. That is, to embrace the truth of your crucifixion and resurrection with Christ.

Many of us are getting on our knees and asking God to make true what is already true. We're saying, "God, give me victory." And God is saying, "I have already given you victory in My Son."

I am free because God says I am free, even when I don't feel as if I'm free. I'm victorious because God says I'm victorious. I need to consider or count it to be true and act like it.

You may say, "Tony, that just sounds like pop psychology, positive thinking." No, it's really more. There's nothing wrong with thinking positively if you're thinking correctly. To think positively about something that's wrong is to think falsely. But to think positively about the truth is good.

We don't have to use our imaginations to think of ourselves as seated with Christ and ruling over Satan. This is our real, present condition as believers.

Children use their imaginations all the time to pretend they're someone else, often a famous person, and they're very good at pretending. They can transport themselves anywhere they want to go and be anybody they want to be.

When kids pretend, they do it with motivation and excitement. But they have no power because it's all make-believe. The little boy in the driveway bouncing a basketball isn't really Michael Jordan.

The difference between this and us as Christians counting ourselves dead to sin and seated in the heavenly places with Christ is that we *do* have power because this is real. What we are considering to be true is really true.

What You Need to Present

Once you know the truth about your position and that fact has settled down into your heart and mind so that you have really grasped it, you're ready to do something about it.

The action that God wants His people to take is stated first negatively, and then positively, in Romans 6:13: "Do not go on presenting the members of your body to sin as instruments of unrighteousness; but present yourselves to God as those alive from the dead, and your bodies as instruments of righteousness to God."

Since we died to sin with Christ, and came alive from the dead when He came alive, we can do something about it when sin wants to take control of our bodies.

When that addiction shows up, when the taste for alcohol comes on strong, or when we are tempted to abandon our biblical responsibility, we can go to God and say, "Lord, I know that in Jesus Christ I am more than a conqueror. I don't feel like a conqueror, but I am presenting my body to You because I know You can give me the power I need to resist and be victorious."

In other words, when sin shows up you need to hold a worship service. Presenting your body to God is an act of worship, according to Romans 12:1. Paul wrote, "Therefore I urge you, brethren, by the mercies of God, to present your bodies a living and holy sacrifice, acceptable to God, which is your spiritual service of worship."

Why does God want the members of our bodies presented to Him as sacrifices and instruments of righteousness? Because for any sin we commit, we are going to have to use some part of our bodies to commit it. The same is true when we act righteously. Whether it's our eyes or hands or feet or mouths, or even our minds, we express ourselves through our bodies.

Whenever you present yourself to God, you call on God's power and God's life to become activated in you. But remember, you must die to sin and be resurrected before you can live to righteousness. That's why you also need to hold a private funeral service every morning.

In the morning when you get up, declare, "I am crucified with Christ" (Galatians 2:20). I confess that every morning. I want to be like Paul, who said, "I die daily" (1 Corinthians 15:31). Just a quick funeral. I'm dead, the old me is gone, and the life I now live this day is the life of Jesus Christ.

All of the staff members at our church have computers, but some get more benefit from their computers because they know more. So we had training sessions to help everyone get the most out of the power at their fingertips.

As Christians we have the power of God at our fingertips. But if we don't know what He has done for us, and don't put it into practice, we'll never maximize that power.

Several years ago, the New Orleans Saints football team gave up just about every draft option they had to get Ricky Williams, the star running back from the University of Texas. Their goal was to make Williams into a Saint.

As a collegiate runner, Ricky Williams was one of the greatest of all time. But as of this writing, his career with the Saints has been disappointing—despite the fact that New Orleans gave up everything to make Williams a Saint.

You know where I'm going with this. On the cross of Calvary, Jesus Christ gave everything so we could be saints. But for some of us, our "career" as saints has been disappointing to God. Some saints are fumbling the ball and getting thrown for losses in the backfield.

But no matter what your condition right now, if you're a saint—a Christian—you have the most exalted position in the universe because the price has been paid to make you a saint. Your job, and mine, is to learn how to start acting like the saints we are.

Chapter Four

THE BATTLE WITHIN

Not long ago, something very unusual happened to me. I got the flu and wasn't able to come to the office for a day or two. It's rare for me to be ill. And even when I'm not feeling well, it's even rarer for me to miss work. But this time I was really sick. The flu bug knocked me to my knees, and I was down and out for a while.

The flu that gripped my body and made its effects felt is a good illustration of the spiritual flu of sin that has infected all of us. Not only have we been infected by sin, but many times it has knocked us to our knees.

Such was the condition of the apostle Paul when he wrote the last half of Romans 7, a classic passage on our struggle with sin. Let me state right up front that Paul was writing as a Christian. Throughout these verses, he used the present tense: "I am." This was his current state as a Christian struggling with, and sometimes losing to, sin.

If you have ever struggled to be free of the handcuffs of sin—and every Christian has—then don't feel like you're alone. The greatest Christian who ever lived has been where you are. Paul knew the reality of the battle within.

In the previous chapter, we argued that when you came to Christ, your sin nature died. We described this nature as a "sin factory" that all of us were born with, but that was shut down by the power of Christ when we received Him as Savior.

This raises the question we suggested earlier. If our old nature, the old person we were outside of Christ, died when we accepted Christ, why are we still battling with sin and losing the battle so often? How can sin take us hostage if our sin nature no longer exists? That's the question I need to address in this chapter. Let's talk about the battle that often rages within us.

THE SERIOUSNESS OF THE BATTLE

When you read Romans 7, there is no doubt that Paul knew he was in a battle. He wrote in verse 15, "For what I am doing, I do not understand; for I am not practicing what I would like to do, but I am doing the very thing I hate."

Paul couldn't figure out what was wrong with him. He knew better than to do whatever it was he was struggling with. I believe the details of Paul's problem were left intentionally vague so other believers could identify fully with this passage. Have you ever looked at yourself in the mirror and said, "What in the world is wrong with you? You know you shouldn't be doing what you're doing."

We know this battle was serious for Paul because he hated what he was doing. And he didn't try to justify or excuse it. "If I do the very thing I do not want to do, I agree with the Law, confessing that the Law is good" (Romans 7:16).

Paul readily confessed that he was wrong. He concurred that God's way was the right way. Paul just didn't know how to free himself from his struggle. He was frustrated by the fact that he was not able to please God the way he wanted to and the way he knew he needed to.

You may wonder how this could be true of a believer like Paul. How could the great apostle feel such a battle within? The closer you get to God, the more sensitive you are to the struggle against sin, and the more sensitive you are to your failure.

That's very important to know. Romans 7 is the battle of a person who was pursuing God with such fire and commitment that his failure to please God was more graphically displayed. Don't get discouraged if the closer you try to walk with God, the more aware you are of your sin.

Show me a Christian who does not feel the pain of sin, and I'll show you a carnal Christian. A truly spiritual Christian is pained and frustrated by sin. What Paul was describing is not the remorse of a person who is upset only because he got caught or because he had to suffer negative consequences. Paul was pursuing what is good. He wanted to obey God's Law.

People like this hate to lie because they know God said not to lie. They are pained when they are envious or filled with lust, because they know God is grieved when they do these things. They hate sin, and they hate it when they sin. Sin is like shackles on their hands and feet.

How serious is this struggle with sin? Paul called it a war raging within him, and he felt like a prisoner of that war (Romans 7:23). He fought the battle day after day and week after week, but he was losing more often than he was winning. I'd call that a pretty serious battle, wouldn't you?

If we're new people in Christ and destined for freedom, and yet we're locked in a serious battle, we'd better be finding out where this conflict is coming from. What is the source of the battle within?

THE SOURCE OF THE BATTLE

We touched on this question in the previous chapter when we looked at Romans 6 and concluded something very important. As long as we are on earth, sin will be an issue for us because our new nature, the real us, is still housed in a body contaminated by sin.

The Bible refers to this corrupt shell we're living in as the "flesh." Before we go any further, it's important for you to realize that this is *not* the old sin nature, which has been done away with, but the sin-ravaged bodies we will inhabit until Christ comes for us.

Paul was very clear about the source of the battle that was frustrating and defeating him. It was his flesh. "For we know that the Law is spiritual, but I am of flesh, sold into bondage to sin" (Romans 7:14). "For I know that nothing good dwells in me, that is, in my flesh" (v. 18).

The Factory's Products

To understand the impact that the flesh still has on us, let's go back to our analogy of the old nature as a sin factory that has been shut down so that it is no longer producing sin.

Suppose that General Motors permanently closed all of its automobile plants tomorrow. From then on, there would never be another new GM car rolling off the assembly line.

But even if GM closed and never reopened, we would not immediately be free from all of GM's impact. Why? Because there are still millions of General Motors products out there on the streets.

General Motor's influence would be felt for a long time. The products it has produced over the years have found a place in our society. And all of these vehicles are still operating by the governing principles used to make them.

That's what sin has done with our bodies. Even though our sin nature was put to death in Christ, the sin it produced for all those years has lodged in our flesh. The factory isn't operating anymore, but its effects are still being felt because the principle of sin has a home in our bodies and can still express itself in many ways. It's obvious that a person who has accepted Christ is still capable of sinning, because all of us sin every day in some way. There is still something within us that can respond to temptations to sin—what the Bible calls "sin which dwells in [us]" (Romans 7:20).

That's why the Bible calls our flesh the "body of sin" (Romans 6:6). Our bodies are inhabited by the presence of sin. By the way, this is why it's so important to reach children for Christ early in life, before the sin nature has had time to function for years and turn out too many "products."

Some adult Christians are still reeling from the effects of sins they committed decades ago. But if we can lead children to Christ early and firmly establish them in the faith, they won't have all of that junk to drag with them into adulthood.

So we must understand that sin in our lives as believers is not the expression of our new nature, but a residual effect of the old nature—the products of the old factory. And we must understand the flesh as a mechanism through which sin expresses itself.

The Principle of Sin

We've been talking about sin as if it were an entity in itself, distinct from your true self. It really is, as I will demonstrate below.

For now, we need to see what Paul meant when he said, "But I see a different law in the members of my body, waging war against the law of my mind and making me a prisoner of the law of sin which is in my members" (Romans 7:23).

Notice the two laws Paul says are at work in the lives of believers. The law of sin is at work in our bodies, which is why we won't be taking these bodies to heaven.

Don't misunderstand. The Bible does not say that our bodies are evil in themselves. But they have been so infiltrated by a foreign substance called sin that they cannot be patched up. The other law at work in Christians is what Paul called "the law of my mind." This is a reference to the real you, the new redeemed nature that God placed inside of you when you received Christ as your Savior and were born from above.

The law or principle of sin, the "sin which dwells in me" (v. 20), is a potent force. Back in verses 11–14, Paul said it was sin that was killing him using something good, which was God's law.

Sin is so potent and deceitful it will "piggyback" on the goodness of God to get its way. Paul knew that the Law of God is wholly good and not a source of sin. But sin uses the very commands of God to promote its agenda, because we do not have the power within ourselves to obey God's holy commands.

This is why the problem of sin can never be fixed by trying to keep the Law or resolving to do better. Sin uses the Law to incite us to do wrong.

We can see this with our children. What happens when you tell your child not to touch something? That's laying down the law, but what happens is that your command only psyches your child up to touch the forbidden thing. In fact, that child may not be able to think of anything else.

We could call this the "wet paint" syndrome. The sign is there, saying "Wet Paint: Do Not Touch," but some people just have to reach out and make sure it's wet. The reason we are still tempted to break God's Law even as believers is that the old patterns of sin are still programmed into our flesh. The devil knows that, and he knows how to trigger those reactions.

You are . . . one totally new nature that functions in an old, sin-infested house.

This pattern is so ingrained in human nature that one museum had to change the sign on an exhibit. The museum discovered that its "Do not touch" sign was so ineffective that the antique furniture in the exhibit was being soiled and damaged from people constantly touching it.

The museum staff considered closing the exhibit, but then someone came up with an idea. They changed the sign to read, "Please wash hands after touching exhibit." It worked.

This human bent toward lawbreaking works like jet lag. I know that when I come back home from a trip to Israel, for example, I feel disoriented for several days because I am carrying around in my body the residual effects of the trip.

When you come to Jesus Christ, He transports you immediately to the heavenly places and seats you with Himself at the right hand of God the Father.

But you still carry the residual effects of the trip, because you are still in your body where sin has made itself at home. You are not a person with two natures fighting against one another, but one totally new nature that functions in an old, sin-infested house.

The more you did something, the more it developed into a pattern. The more you thought about something, the more you thought yourself into a pattern. That's why merely trying harder doesn't solve your problem.

I have had many people sit across from me in my office and promise they were going to try hard to do what was right, and they really meant it.

Paul wanted to do right. The desire was there, but the ability wasn't until he understood a principle we'll talk about later. Paul wanted to be free from the shackles of sin, but sin ambushed and dominated him through his flesh.

The Real You Versus Sin

It's important to see that as he wrestled with the reality of sin and the fact of his new nature, Paul distinguished between the two. There are two actors here, not one—the "I" who is not doing it, and the sin that *is* doing it. Twice Paul said that when he did wrong, it wasn't him doing it but "sin which dwells in me" (vv. 17, 20).

That might sound like Paul was shifting the blame for his sin somewhere else. But that's not the case. We can't do something wrong and then claim, "That wasn't me doing that. It was just the sin dwelling in me." We're responsible for our sin, because God has not left us defenseless against sin. Don't ever stop reading Romans 7 too soon. But the battle against sin is very real because sin is very real.

In Genesis 4 we have the familiar story of Cain. After his offering was rejected by God, Cain became angry and God issued him a warning. "If you do well, will not your countenance be lifted up? And if you do not do well, sin is crouching at the door; and its desire is for you, but you must master it" (v. 7).

Cain didn't master sin, of course, and it leaped all over him when he killed his brother Abel.

This is an important passage. God says sin is like a lion crouching, ready to pounce on us and devour us. What's crucial here is that sin is a noun, not a verb.

You may say, "So what? What does grammar have to do with the battle?" Everything! You see, if sin is just a verb then we can talk about it merely in terms of the things we do. For example, if a person says, "My problem is that I tell lies," then the focus is on his need to change his actions and stop lying.

But we've already seen that just trying to be good, even trying very hard, is not enough because it doesn't get to the root of the problem. Recognizing that "I tell lies" is a lot different from admitting, "I am a liar. The sin of lying has pounced on me and is devouring me. I am being controlled by the principle of sin."

Of course, when the entity, or we could say the "noun," of sin pounces on us, it will produce the actions of sin in our lives. But only dealing with the actions is like bandaging up your wounds while a lion is still clawing you. Someone needs to get that lion.

A liar's real problem is not just that he tells lies, as serious as that is. Lying is just the expression of his problem, which is that sin has mastered him in this area.

Sin expresses itself in a myriad of sinful activities, but the activities are not the root of sin. They are the fruit of sin. We have a "noun problem" called sin, a lion called sin that we must overcome. This is the source of the battle, and it's all too real because there's a real being inside the lion's suit—our Enemy, the devil (see 1 Peter 5:8).

THE STRATEGY OF THE BATTLE

Maybe this would be a good time to take a step back and review where we've been and where we're going. At this point, you may not feel like a new person who is destined for freedom because we have been concentrating pretty heavily on the battle.

But it's vital that we do this, or we won't be prepared to handle the Enemy's arsenal when he unloads it on us. It's still possible for us to be mastered by sin in our daily experience. So we need to ask and answer the question, how does sin try to master us? What strategy does the Enemy use to attack us?

Gathering the Information

A very helpful analogy for me is that of a football team studying films of its opponent in order to develop a game plan for that opponent.

Every team does this. The coaches and players study the game film over and over again, looking for any weakness or idiosyncrasy in the other team that they can exploit to their advantage.

Similarly, Satan and his demons are studying your "game film." They know your desires and habits and the patterns you have established. They know your tendencies and your weaknesses, so when the devil and his demons sit down to plan a strategy against you, they know where to hit you for maximum effect. They know where you are vulnerable.

Formulating a Plan

Once Satan has gathered this information, he devises a battle strategy.

One reason Satan's strategies against us work so well is that he knows us. But there's another factor at work. As Satan launches his attack against us he also has an ally, a traitor, behind the lines—the entity of sin that dwells in our flesh.

To change the analogy, Satan sends out signals that are collected by the receiver in our bodies called sin. Satan's signals are tuned to our faults and weaknesses, and the receiver picks up the signals and tells our flesh what to focus on. It's a very simple and effective strategy.

Keeping Sin a Verb

This is why the devil wants you to keep treating sin as a verb instead of a noun.

By that, I mean he wants to keep you focused on trying to stop doing certain things. If you say, "I have a problem with a sinful activity, and I need to work on it," he's got you. The action may be a problem, for sure, but it could also prevent you from working on the cause of the problem. We need to deal with the entity of indwelling sin, the traitor behind the lines that is aiding and abetting Satan's plan.

We said back at the beginning of our study that one of Satan's favorite strategies is to plant his thoughts in your mind so completely that you come to believe they are your thoughts. Then you begin to act on those thoughts.

We know why this strategy works so well. Satan has an ally within us called indwelling sin that helps him bombard us with his evil thoughts. But sin keeps a low profile, getting us to think in terms of *I*, *me*, and *my*, so we come to own the problem as if it were our own. But in Romans 7, Paul was careful to make the distinction between his new nature and the sin principle.

Again, someone may raise the question, "Well, if Satan is sending me these sinful thoughts, then how can I be blamed for acting on them?" Because you and I are responsible for what we do with these thoughts once they enter our minds. This is why the Bible says we must be active in "taking every thought captive to the obedience of Christ" (2 Corinthians 10:5).

When an evil thought comes, we have two choices. We can reject it, or we can adopt it and make it part of the family. You aren't responsible for a thought until you have adopted it. Then it becomes yours.

That's why it is not a sin to be tempted. Satan can introduce a thought and entice you with it, but you don't have to adopt it. Realize that evil thoughts are not coming from you, because you are a new person with a new nature, and your new nature will never think anything that is contrary to Christ.

Satan will always try to personalize sin so you will think it's coming from you. That's why he is called the deceiver.

THE SOLUTION TO THE BATTLE

I said earlier that you don't ever want to quit reading Romans 7 too early. That's because the last two verses contain the solution to the battle within us.

In verse 24, Paul summarized all that he had said about the battle with sin when he cried out, "Wretched man that I am! Who will set me free from the body of this death?" A better way to translate that last phrase is "this body of death." It's a reference to the sin-contaminated flesh we've been talking about.

Powerless on Our Own

Here Paul admitted something that a lot of Christians today aren't willing to admit. He admitted he was powerless to resolve his problem (see Romans 7:15–16, 19). All through Romans 7 he tried to get the upper hand on sin, but he couldn't pull it off on his own. If you have ever been hopelessly in debt, you have an idea how Paul felt.

To Paul, having to live in his sinful flesh was like dragging a dead body around with him. If you know someone whose arm or leg has been rendered useless by an accident or disease, or someone who is paralyzed and wheelchair-bound, you know what a trial it can be for that person. Whenever Jesus met crippled people, they wanted to be healed.

All of us, whether we're disabled or not, carry around with us the crippling effects of our sinful flesh, these bodies destined for death. We may carry anger around inside of us day after day, or the pain of hurts that happened years ago.

We may even say, "I don't want to keep dragging around this anger. I don't want to keep on hurting from things in my past. I don't want to be a slave to this addiction. But I don't know how to get free. Who will set me free from this body of death?"

We have to come to this point before we are ready for the solution to the battle. As long as we think we can do it ourselves, we'll find the dead weight of our old body of sin dragging us down.

Powerful in Christ

The battle is great, but the solution is infinitely greater!

After his intense struggle with indwelling sin, Paul burst forth in praise in Romans 7:25. "Thanks be to God through Jesus Christ our Lord!" You can almost hear the apostle shouting it out in triumph. As powerless as Paul was in himself, he was that much more powerful in Christ (see 2 Corinthians 12:10).

You say, "Tony, that sounds great! I'm ready to admit I can't do it on my own. How do I find the solution to the battle that Paul found?"

The key to the solution isn't stated here in so many words, but it is implied and wrapped up in Paul's simple confession of Christ. The solution is not found simply in turning to Jesus Christ for your help but in turning your life over to Him completely. Let me show you what I mean.

In Colossians 3:4, Paul referred to Christ as "our life." That's a profound statement, because it means Jesus Christ did not come merely to be our helper, our divine assistant. He did not come just to take part in our lives but to take over our lives.

You see, if all you want is a little help and a little boost from Jesus to get you over the top, you'll never make it. You'll never have victory. You won't find the solution to the battle within, you won't be free at last, until Jesus becomes your life. He must become the definition of who you are.

Here's an illustration of what I'm saying. If you discovered that pests had infiltrated your kitchen, you could do one of two things. The first solution would be to take off your shoe or grab a flyswatter and go to war against the roaches or ants or whatever was crawling across your kitchen floor.

Bam! Whop! You could kill every bug you see. You could stand guard in your kitchen all night, declaring, "I am not going to let these roaches take over my house!"

I'm sure you know that would be a huge waste of time, because just killing the insects you can see doesn't solve your problem. By the time you get one or two, the others have scattered. And besides, that doesn't deal with the unseen insects in the wall that are producing more insects.

But this is the way a lot of us approach our sin problems. We say, "I'm going to try to get rid of my anger today." So we wait for a "roach" of anger to show up, and Bam! We give it a good swat. Or we wait for lust to show its ugly face, and Whop! We try to smash it. But the problem keeps coming back because we haven't gotten to the heart of the problem.

The second solution to a bug problem is to call in a professional. If you have a problem with roaches, you need somebody who has the equipment and chemicals to penetrate the crevices of your house and solve your problem at its source. You don't need a helper to swat roaches with you. You need somebody with the power to eradicate those bad boys.

Now I don't know about you, but I have never had a professional exterminator ask me to help him do his job. My only assignment is to get out of the way and let him do his thing. In fact, depending on how bad a bug problem is, the homeowner may even have to leave the house.

If you'll allow me to apply the illustration this way, we could paraphrase Paul by saying, "O, roach-infested Christian that I am! Who will deliver me from this terrible infestation?"

The answer to the infestation of sin is to exchange my life for Christ's life, to let Him be my life. That means I say, "Lord, I want You to be my life."

Jesus doesn't want to be your assistant. He wants to be your *life*, your identity. He wants to be the sum total of who you are. When He becomes your all, you can cry out in triumph, "Thanks be to God through Jesus Christ my Lord!" He is the solution to the battle within.

Chapter Five

THE EXCHANGED LIFE

One of the crimes that's growing fast in our high-tech, information-driven society is known as identity theft. This happens when someone gets hold of another person's credit information and other personal data and uses these to make expensive purchases and carry out other transactions in the victim's name.

This crime is well named because as far as the credit and banking systems are concerned, the person using the information is the same person whose name is on the card or account. For all practical purposes, there has been an exchange of identity.

What identity thieves accomplish illegitimately, Jesus Christ has accomplished legitimately for believers. That is, He has effected an exchange of identity with you. Christ did not simply come to change your life. He came to *exchange* your life for His. And when we understand this, we are on our way to being free at last.

I'm convinced the reason a lot of Christians don't experience the abundant life Jesus came to give (John 10:10) is that they don't understand the truth of the exchanged life. It's not that these believers don't want the fullness of joy, peace, and power that Jesus gives. They just don't know how to find it. The problem is that too many of us are trying to live the Christian life. That's not a contradiction, because the Christian life is, by definition, the life of Christ. And He's the only person who has ever lived the Christian life successfully.

So in order for you and me to live the Christian life, Christ must live His life in and through us while we get out of the way. That's what we mean by the exchanged life.

This concept is captured and capsulized in Galatians 2:20, a verse we have encountered several times. This is Paul's spiritual declaration of independence, his emancipation proclamation. I want to break this verse into its component statements and show you what the exchanged life involves.

A CRUCIFIXION

The exchanged life begins with a death experience. Paul opens Galatians 2:20 by declaring, "I have been crucified with Christ." To put it another way, Paul was a dead man walking.

Before we go any further, we need to look at the context of this verse because it's helpful to our understanding of our identity in Christ. Verse 20 is part of Paul's rebuke to Peter for his wrong actions (vv. 11–21).

Don't Forget Who You Are

Peter came down to Antioch and started fellowshiping with his Gentile brothers. But when some of Peter's Jewish "homeboys" from Jerusalem showed up and saw him hanging out on the wrong side of the tracks, Peter got up and left the Gentile believers sitting there so as not to offend his Jewish brethren.

But Paul saw what Peter did and became "evangelically" ticked off. He confronted Peter because Peter was acting contrary to the gospel and leading other Jews to do the same, making the Gentile believers feel like second-class citizens in the kingdom. Everything was wrong with Peter's actions.

You can read Paul's rebuke for yourself. Basically, he said to

Peter, "You're confused about who you are. On one hand, you're saying you're a Christian and racial differences don't matter. But what you're doing contradicts your message."

A Christian who preaches one thing and does something else has an identity problem. Peter temporarily lost sight of the fact that he had been crucified with Christ and was now a dead man walking. His life was no longer his to live as he pleased.

Hold a Memorial Service

If we are going to experience the exchanged life, we must first come to terms with our death. When people lose a loved one, they not only hold a funeral service, but they often go to the grave and leave flowers in memory of the dead person. Doing this is part of coming to grips with the death that has occurred.

Maybe that's what we should do as Christians. Let's visit the gravesite of our old selves and leave some flowers, so to speak. Stand there for a few minutes and then leave. We need to do whatever helps us come to grips with the reality that the person we used to be died with Christ on the cross.

The verb in this opening statement of Galatians 2:20 is in a particular form that means it's a "done deal" with lasting effects. Our crucifixion with Christ has already taken place. We're not dual personalities living double lives.

You may say, "But I don't feel crucified." That's all right. Dead people don't feel dead. But you are crucified because God says you're crucified, whether you feel it or not.

This is why Paul could say his only boast was "in the cross of our Lord Jesus Christ" (Galatians 6:14). Paul rejoiced in the cross not just because it meant that his sins were paid for, but because the old Paul—the hate-filled persecutor of the church—was dead and gone. Paul was eager to share in Christ's death so that he might share in His resurrection life.

Leave the Shackles Buried

On August 1, 1831, Jamaican slaves were set free. The slaves gathered to celebrate. A few of the men took shovels and dug a large pit. Someone brought some coffins, and all the slaves took the shackles and chains of their slavery and threw them into the coffins. The coffins were then buried in the pit to symbolize and celebrate the fact that these people were no longer slaves.

It would have been foolish for those freed slaves to go back to that pit and dig up their old shackles so they could wear them again. And yet, we know from history that some freed slaves did actually want to stay with their old masters.

Why? Even though they were free in their bodies, they were not yet free in their minds. So they did the only thing they knew how to do; they acted as if they were still in slavery.

When you died with Christ, you were set free from your old life. But if you don't believe and act like you're free, then you're still a slave. When Jesus Christ exchanged His life for yours, He gave you permission to let go of the old and embrace the new person you are in Him. Christ gave you permission to take His identity with all of its privileges and benefits.

A TRANSMUTATION

A second fact about the exchanged life is that it involves a transmutation. That's a big word that means something has changed from one form to another, usually to a higher form.

Let's go back to Galatians 2:20, where the apostle Paul said that since he had been crucified with Christ, "it is no longer I who live, but Christ lives in me." That's a change of essence, a transmutation—an exchanged life.

A New Resident in an Old House

When you trusted Jesus Christ as your Savior, a notice was served on the old you that read, "You are being evicted. You don't live here anymore because you are dead, and we don't want your corpse around here stinking up the place for the new resident."

You may say, "But I don't feel like I have a new resident. I still have all these problems. I still feel the pull of the world, the flesh, and the devil."

That's because while you have a new resident, Jesus Christ, you still reside in the old house of your sin-contaminated flesh. It has the same old spiritually leaky windows and stained walls and beat-up doors. As long as you are in this flesh, you will still be susceptible to desires and habits that don't please God.

But it won't always be this way. I love 2 Corinthians 5:1, which says an "urban renewal" project is on the way for our bodies. "For we know that if the earthly tent which is our house is torn down, we have a building from God, a house not made with hands, eternal in the heavens."

Christ can shine through our flawed humanity.

Our bodies are like an old, worn-out tent that is going to be taken down for the last time someday and discarded. When the ground has been cleared, then we will be ready for our new eternal bodies that will live forever in heaven. You see, we exchanged our old lives for Christ's new life at the cross, and when He returns we will exchange our old bodies for new ones.

Do you ever get tired of carrying this old body of sin around with you and wish for your new one? I think all Christians feel that way. Let me encourage you by pointing out that God is accomplishing an important purpose in our bodies.

For this we go to Paul again, this time to 2 Corinthians 4:10. The Bible says we are "always carrying about in the body the dying of Jesus, so that the life of Jesus also may be manifested in our body." We display the life of Jesus to the world when we live exchanged lives.

This means that our bodies, our present lives, are to be a daily advertisement for the power and glory of Jesus Christ. The miracle of the exchanged life is that Christ can shine through our flawed humanity.

We could also compare our new life in Christ to what happens to a snail's shell. When a snail dies, its shell remains behind on the ocean floor. The shell still moves around, but only because it's stirred by the currents. It has no life in it.

Hermit crabs, on the other hand, move from shell to shell as they grow. When a hermit crab finds an empty snail shell, it moves in and the shell begins to move again because it has new life within it.

I'm using as many analogies as I can for this concept to help you see how completely Jesus Christ takes over when He comes in. When you were born in Adam, you were a spiritual snail. But when you became a Christian, the snail died. When Jesus Christ inhabited your body, you received new life.

All You Will Ever Need

That's why the Bible says in Colossians 3:4 that Christ is our life. We ended the previous chapter with this verse, which is so crucial to understand if we are going to enjoy the freedom Christ purchased for us.

How can two Christians have Christ in them, and yet one be consistently victorious in the spiritual life while the other is consistently defeated? The difference is that Christ *is* the first Christian's life, while He is just *in* the second Christian's life.

When I exchange my life for Christ's life, He expresses Himself in me. When I think, Christ thinks through me. When I move, Christ moves through me. When I speak, Christ speaks through me. A complete transmutation has occurred. That's why the Bible says that Christ is the fullness of God "in bodily form, and in Him you have been made complete" (Colossians 2:9–10). He is all you will ever need.

I'm amazed when I go to one of our "supercenters" here in the Dallas area. These stores have everything you need. Want to get your film developed? Bring it with you. Need to cash a check? They'll cash a check for you. You can also rent a video or buy a book, fill your prescription or get new glasses, and purchase some fertilizer and a sprinkler for your lawn—all while having your car serviced, in some cases. You can buy your groceries too. Thanks to the supercenter, I don't have to drive all over the neighborhood meeting my needs.

You know where I'm going with this. You are complete in Christ. Do you need wisdom? Come to your "super Savior." Do you need direction in your life? Come to your super Savior. The same is true for your physical needs, burdens, family problems, or anything else. Whatever you need, Christ is because He is God, and He is your life.

You may feel powerless, and you *are* in yourself. That's why a change, a transmutation, must take place. You need to exchange your weakness for Christ's strength.

You've seen those truck commercials showing a truck pulling a big boat or a camper uphill. You never see that boat struggling to make it uphill. It's already hooked up to the power source, which is built into the truck. The power source for the Christian is Christ. All you have to do is make sure you are properly connected to Him.

AN EXPECTATION

You may be reading this, scratching your head, and saying, "Tony, all of this sounds good. But it's not working for me. I pray and read my Bible. I go to church and try to witness. I'm doing the right things, but I'm not seeing this victory you're talking about. What's wrong?"

Let me suggest an answer, based on the next section of our key verse in Galatians 2:20. The exchanged life involves an expectation as well as a crucifixion and a transmutation. Paul continued, "The life which I now live in the flesh I live by faith in the Son of God."

Putting the Engine Up Front

There it is. God's expectation is that we will live this new life by faith. The exchanged life, the life of freedom in Christ, is activated *only* by faith. Not by trying or straining or even praying. If we expect to see the life of Christ truly activated in us, we must live by faith.

I have a very simple definition of faith: Faith is living as if God is telling the truth. The essence of faith is taking God at His word. We've emphasized all the way through that our identity with Christ, and all that goes with it, is true—whether we feel like it or not—because God's Word says it's true.

The great thing about faith is that you can operate by faith regardless of how you feel. Feelings have no necessary relationship to faith because faith deals with your feet, not with your "feel." That's an important distinction.

We don't have to deny our emotions to activate our faith. We just need to get the two in the right order. Someone has likened faith to the engine of a train, with feelings as the caboose. They're linked, but you can't operate a train from the caboose.

When I hear people say, "Well, I feel this way or that way," I'm not necessarily going to try to convince them that what they're feeling isn't real. What I want them to see is that our emotions were never meant to be the measure by which we live.

That's true, by the way, whether our emotions are good and strong and healthy, uplifting us or pulling us down. Paul's confidence was in Christ, not in himself.

When He was on earth, Jesus gave us an example of what it means to live with total confidence in God. Jesus depended totally on the Father for everything He did and everything He said (see John 5:30; 12:49; 14:10). Even though Jesus is fully God, He didn't make one move without His Father's direction. The Lord isn't asking us to do anything He didn't do Himself.

What God Can Do Through You

What can happen when we start living by faith in the Son of God, letting Him live His life through us? Let me give you a practical example.

Think of the person you have the hardest time relating to. It could be someone who has hurt you deeply or wronged you but who needs the Lord. After you think of this person, you can offer this prayer in faith: "Lord, You know I feel no love for this person. You know that in my flesh, I have already rejected this person. Lord, You know the truth. You know that without Your help, I can't forgive or accept or love this person.

"But I know You love my enemy, so right now I give You permission to express Your love and care and forgiveness for this person through me. I give You permission to use my flawed humanity as the vehicle through which You reach out to this person. I can't do this myself, but I'm going to trust You to love this person through me."

Once you start really living like this, putting faith ahead of feelings, things are going to start happening. You're going to see God do things in your life you didn't think possible.

Let me caution you, it may feel awkward at first if you're not used to living by faith. But that's OK, because we can get comfortable doing things we felt awkward doing at first.

Most people have done this in regard to sin. Many alcoholics can probably testify that those first few drinks tasted strong, or burned their throat, or made them sick. But eventually drinking became second nature to them. Many drug addicts were probably scared the first time they used drugs. But their bodies became accustomed to the drugs. If people can become so used to sinning that it's second nature to them, we can learn to live by faith until it's as natural as breathing to us.

We are crucified with Christ and He is living His life through us.

Remember the singing group Milli Vanilli? They were a big sensation until someone exposed them as a fake because the guys were lip-synching instead of singing themselves. I'd like to suggest that there's a lesson here for us. Instead of trying to lip-synch the Christian life, faking our way through while mouthing all the right words, God wants us to "life-synch" the Christian life. That is, He wants us to imitate Him completely, becoming the mind and mouth and hands and feet through which He expresses Himself.

There's a big difference between a pole-vaulter and a high jumper. A high jumper does it all by human effort, leaping as high as he possibly can. A good high jumper can clear seven feet.

But a pole-vaulter flies a lot higher because he has something going for himself besides his two legs. He has a pole in his hands that has both the ability to bear his weight and the strength to catapult him over a bar that is twenty feet or more above the ground.

Do you want to be a high-jumping Christian or a pole-vaulting Christian? If you want to soar higher than you've ever soared before, get hold of Jesus Christ and, by faith, put all your weight on Him.

A MOTIVATION

Here's a fourth reality about the exchanged life. It involves a motivation that grows out of the fact that we are crucified with Christ and He is living His life through us.

Paul concluded Galatians 2:20 by talking about what Christ had done for him. "[He] loved me, and delivered Himself up for me." Given that kind of sacrificial love, how can we do less than give ourselves wholly to Christ, letting Him live through us? It's our "spiritual service of worship" (Romans 12:1).

Saved by Christ's Life

The motivation also goes the other way. If Christ loved us enough to give His life *for* us, then He loves us enough to give His life *to* us so that He might express His life *through* us.

The Bible says we are saved by the life of Christ, not just by His death. "For if while we were enemies we were reconciled to God through the death of His Son, much more, having been reconciled, we shall be saved by His life" (Romans 5:10).

That may sound curious. How are we saved by Christ's life? The reason is that His perfect life on earth qualified Jesus Christ to be the perfect sacrifice for our sins on the cross. God demanded total obedience to His Law, which no one but Jesus ever achieved.

For thirty-three years, Jesus fulfilled every demand of the Law. So His sacrifice on the cross perfectly satisfied God's judgment against sin forever. My sins will never be brought up in heaven, because Jesus Christ paid the penalty.

Why is that important to you today? Because when you exchange your life with the Christ who died for you and rose from the dead, He brings to you the power of His perfect, sinless life to enable you to be victorious.

Victory in Jesus

Let me show you what I mean. The Bible says Jesus has already faced every kind of temptation you and I will ever experience (see Hebrews 4:15).

Imagine what that means. It doesn't matter what you're going through right now. It doesn't matter how hard the world, the flesh, and the devil are bombarding you, Jesus has been there and understands what you're up against.

And because Jesus defeated every temptation, He can provide you all the power you need to defeat your temptations. That's why the author of Hebrews goes on to tell us, "Draw near with confidence to the throne of grace, so that we may receive mercy and find grace to help in time of need" (Hebrews 4:16).

This is how we are saved by Jesus' life. His death gets us from earth to heaven, but His life brings heaven down to earth. Jesus not only died to get you to glory, He died so that glory could come down to you. There is nothing Jesus hasn't been victorious over, and He wants to transfer that victory to you.

That's all the motivation we need to live the exchanged life. The victory is that Christ loves you so much He died to take you to heaven and lives to replace your weakness with His strength.

And when you allow Him to express His life through you, you get the victory and God gets the glory. The Cross is not only about forgiving your sins but about delivering life to you.

The story is told of a man who lived alone in a small town. The man took in a boy who had become an orphan and didn't have anyplace to go, and over time the man grew to love the boy as his own son.

One day, the man's house was engulfed in fire. The boy was trapped in the house, and the man fought desperately to save him. The man managed to save the boy's life, but in the process his hands were badly burned.

Sometime later, some distant relatives of the boy showed up in the town, demanding to take custody of the boy. The case went to trial, and the judge asked the man if he had any legal papers to prove he had adopted the boy. The man replied that he had none. "Then why should I give you custody of this boy? How do I know you will love him and care for him properly?" the judge asked. The man stood quietly and held out his badly scarred hands. The judge ruled in his favor.

There is a Man in heaven whose scarred hands prove His love for you and me. He has won custody of us forever, and the scars He received on the cross are also evidence that He is perfectly capable of caring for us today. Jesus wants to exchange His perfect life for your struggles and failures. When you make that transaction, you will be free at last.

Chapter Six

THE BONDAGE OF LEGALISM

A man who had been born and raised in a country ruled by a strict military dictatorship immigrated to the United States and became a citizen of this country.

The man decided to celebrate his new U.S. citizenship by doing some sight-seeing around the city where he was living. He was enjoying himself so much he didn't notice that sundown was approaching. But as soon as the sunlight faded and darkness began to descend on the city, the new American panicked.

He ran up to a man in a car and begged the driver to take him home as quickly as possible. The driver was taken aback and tried to calm the man. When asked why he had to get home so quickly, the man cried out, "Because I don't want to violate curfew and be arrested."

The problem was that in the man's previous country, the military had imposed a strict curfew. Everyone had to be off the streets by sundown or risk arrest.

The man in the car smiled when he realized the problem. He

calmly explained that since the U.S. has no curfew, the man wasn't going to be in trouble for staying out past sundown. The new citizen simply had not yet learned to cast off the bondage of the old country. He was free, but he wasn't living like it.

Most of us can't even imagine living under a regime that dictates every detail of its citizens' lives. And I doubt if we could find many people who would choose to place themselves in such legal bondage when they can be citizens of a free country.

But this is exactly what a lot of Christians have done. They are citizens of heaven and possess freedom in Christ, but for some reason they have not learned how to cast off the bondage of their birth in Adam. They sing and talk about freedom, but they are living under an oppressive system of religious rules that sends them running home at sundown, so to speak. There's a name for this way of life, this oppressive religious system. It's called legalism, and it's contrary to the freedom we have through our identity with Christ. Unfortunately, many Christians are being held hostage to the old regime.

If there is one truth I wish I could get across to Christians bound in legalism, it would be this: When we got saved, we were brought into a new regime. The old rules no longer apply. "He [God] rescued us from the domain of darkness, and transferred us to the kingdom of His beloved Son" (Colossians 1:13).

I realize that applying the truth we know can be another story, especially when it comes to an issue such as legalism. Law-keeping can exert a strong pull on us, so we need to see what legalism is and how it shackles us before we can understand how to break its chains.

The Bible goes to great lengths to combat legalism and establish us in grace. If you are a legalist, you will never enjoy grace or know real spiritual freedom. If you are a legalist, the Christian life will be a burden to you, not a joy. So let's find out how to shed the shackles.

THE CONCEPT OF LEGALISM

What exactly is legalism in the spiritual realm? We have a definition in Galatians 3:3, stated in the form of a question. Paul asked the Galatians, "Having begun by the Spirit, are you now being perfected by the flesh?"

Legalism is trying to please God "by the flesh," by attempting to keep a list of laws and rules that we think will earn us God's favor and keep us in good standing with Him. It is identity based on performance rather than relationship. It makes rule-keeping the basis of victory. It says you are what you do.

A Different Message

The problem with this should be obvious. We can't earn our salvation. We didn't begin with Christ by doing works of the flesh, but by the grace of God administered by the Holy Spirit. Paul's question demands a negative reply. We cannot begin the Christian life by grace and then live it by legalism.

This is such a serious matter that Paul used the strongest language possible in addressing the Galatians, who had fallen victim to legalism. He began his letter by saying, "I am amazed that you are so quickly deserting Him who called you by the grace of Christ, for a different gospel" (Galatians 1:6).

Legalism is so antithetical to grace that it is a completely different concept. Notice that even though Paul called legalism a "gospel," he was using the word to shock his readers. He quickly added that it was not really another gospel but a distortion of the true gospel (v. 7).

We need to remember that wherever Paul went, he was followed by Jewish teachers called Judaizers who sought to subject Gentile Christians to the Law of Moses. It was an attempt to put them under the bondage of a system that no one but Jesus ever kept. These Judaizers were the people troubling the Galatians (1:7).

The problem was that these "false brethren" had come to Galatia "to spy out our liberty which we have in Christ Jesus, in order to bring us into bondage" (Galatians 2:4). This was serious, because Paul later said these false teachers would bear God's judgment (5:10).

This is why he used such strong language. "You foolish Galatians, who has bewitched you, before whose eyes Jesus Christ was publicly portrayed as crucified?" (3:1). The answer to that question was the Judaizers.

A Few Good Questions

Then Paul asked another series of questions in Galatians 3:2–5, all of which contrast grace or faith with works. The correct answer in each case is that the Christian life, symbolized by the giving of the Holy Spirit, is a matter of Grace and not of works.

Allow me to ask you a few questions. Were you saved by keeping the Ten Commandments? Are you going to heaven because you're better than your neighbor? Are you hoping to please God by trying your very hardest to be good?

I hope the answer to each of these questions is no, because no one will ever be saved or make it to heaven or please God by these means. When you try to mix human effort with God's grace, you're trying to mix oil and water. It will never work.

Paul was asking, "Foolish Galatians, what makes you think you can be saved by grace and then be set free by trying to keep the Law? What makes you think the Holy Spirit is good enough to get you started, but not good enough to keep you going?"

Legalism bases our spiritual identity on our performance. It makes rule-keeping the basis of spiritual victory. Don't misunderstand me. Legalism is not merely the *presence* of rules or laws. Earlier we learned that God's Law is "holy and righteous and good" (Romans 7:12). The problem is that the Law provides no power to obey it.

Grace-based Christians obey because it's their delight.

Legalism is not the presence of rules, but the wrong *attitude* toward the rules. Legalism assigns to the rules an authority that God never meant them to have. You have probably met unsaved people who thought they were good enough to go to heaven. You have to show them otherwise before they are ready to believe and receive the gospel.

What is true of the sinner who is trying to make it to heaven is true of a saint who is trying to be victorious. Victory and true liberty cannot be found in human efforts to keep the rules.

A Guilt-Driven System

You see, legalism is a guilt-motivated system. We either allow others to put us in bondage to their list of rules, or we shackle ourselves to our own list. The more guilty we feel, the more rules we add to the list and the harder we try to keep them.

Here's how it works: A Christian who tends toward legalism goes to church one Sunday and hears the preacher say, "You need to read your Bible and pray."

This Christian feels guilty because he hasn't been reading his Bible or praying. So he says, "You know, the preacher's right. I ought to be reading my Bible and praying every day." So that night he sets his alarm ahead an hour.

But when the alarm goes off the next morning, this guy doesn't really want to get up. In fact, he's kind of grumpy, but he dutifully staggers out of bed because he feels like he has to. Is there anything wrong with a preacher telling his people they ought to read their Bibles and pray? I hope not, because I'll be the first one to say it. And it's not necessarily bad that this Christian felt guilty over his neglect of his Bible and prayer life. That could be the conviction of the Holy Spirit. The problem comes in the way he deals with his need.

You can always tell a legalist, because to a legalist everything in the Christian life is "I ought" or "I should" instead of "I want to."

Grace-based Christians obey because it's their delight. Law-based Christians obey because it's their duty. Obedience is certainly our duty as Christians, but duty alone without love behind it can degenerate into routine. Grace-based Christians obey and love it. Law-based Christians obey and come to resent it.

To grace-based Christians, the spiritual life is the lifting of a burden. Jesus said, "My burden is light" (Matthew 11:30). But to legalistic Christians, living for God feels like carrying a heavy load. Interestingly, Peter called the Law a "yoke" that none of the Jews was able to bear (Acts 15:10).

Suppose both partners in a marriage carried around checklists of each other's duties in the marriage and checked each duty off as it was done. If the whole marriage was on that basis, I'd soon be seeing that couple in my office for counseling, because marriage can't be reduced to a checklist.

Do husbands and wives who love each other help each other? Of course. But the doing has to grow out of the loving. God wants nothing less from us. If your Christian life is just a list, you're missing it—not necessarily because the things on your list are bad. It's just that living by a list is a faulty approach to the Christian life and a faulty approach to victory. My prayer is that the Holy Spirit will use the truth to set you free so you can tear up your list. That's going to be difficult if you've been conditioned to live by rules, but you can do it with God's help.

THE CONFUSION BEHIND LEGALISM

Now that we know something about the nature of legalism, we need to ask an important question: If spiritual legalism is so confining and restricting and guilt-producing, why are so many Christians falling into this trap?

In many cases, the answer is that believers are confused about a fundamental truth of the Christian life. Paul stated this truth in Romans 6:14 when he wrote, "Sin shall not be master over you, for you are not under law, but under grace."

A lot of Christians would jump up at this point and object. "Come on, Tony, I know that. That's one of the most basic principles of the Christian life. I'm not confused about that."

We Are Truly Free

But I have to wonder how many believers really understand grace, since so many of God's people are in bondage to some form of legalism. You see, if we really understood grace, then we would realize we are truly free to follow Christ. But freedom scares some folk, like the freed slaves who wanted to stay with their slave masters because slavery was all they had ever known.

God wants us to understand that we are completely *free* from the Law. Not free to live any way we want, because the Law indeed tells us what God wants from us, but free from trying to save ourselves by measuring up to God's perfect standard.

We looked at the second half of Romans 7 in an earlier chapter, so this time I want to go back and pick up the first half because it relates to legalism. In verses 1–4, Paul used the death of a spouse to illustrate our freedom from the Law. A woman whose husband has died is free to remarry. Her obligation to her first marriage ended when her husband died.

The parallel to the believer and the Law is made in verse 4. "Therefore, my brethren, you also were made to die to the Law through the body of Christ, so that you might be joined to another, to Him who was raised from the dead, in order that we might bear fruit for God." The Law was our old "husband," but that relationship is dead, and we are now joined in a new union with Christ.

An Absurd Way to Live

My friend, this means that a Christian who is trying to please God by legalism while joined to Christ in grace is living an absurdity, an impossibility. Let me illustrate what I mean.

Maybe you've heard of the woman who was married to a very strict, demanding man who had a list of rules for her to follow without deviation. Her life was very frustrating, although her husband was at heart a good man who never asked her to do anything wrong. It's just that he had a rule for everything, and she was always tense because she was always trying to meet his expectations.

Well, after decades of marriage, this woman became so used to living by her husband's rules that when he died, she panicked. She didn't know how to function on her own without her husband, so she had him embalmed and took him back home. Worse yet, she still asked the corpse every day for permission to do anything.

But this woman finally decided to get away, so she took a vacation to Europe and met a wonderful man. He treated her kindly, showing her great tenderness and love. She discovered she did things for this man not because she had to but because she wanted to. They fell in love, decided to get married, and agreed to come back to the United States and live in her house.

When the happy newlyweds arrived home, however, the new husband's jaw dropped when he saw the corpse of the woman's first husband on the sofa. The woman quickly explained, "I love you, darling, but you must understand I lived with this man for so long I can't really function without him. I need to keep him nearby."

The woman's new husband let her know in no uncertain terms that he wasn't about to live with a dead man in the house. She would have to choose between her deceased former husband and her new love. I told you this was an absurdity! But this is what we do spiritually when we try to live by the Law after Christ has forgiven and received us by grace. Let's bury that corpse and move on, because mixing law and grace will never work.

God's Good Law

If many believers are confused about the true relationship between Law and grace, some are also confused about the nature and the role of God's Law.

The first thing we need to restate and reinforce is that the problem is not in the Law itself. As we saw earlier, Paul affirmed, "The Law is holy, and the commandment is holy and righteous and good" (Romans 7:12). Congress may enact some bad laws, but not God.

So the Law of God is good, every word of it. But if it can't save us, what is its purpose? Why did God give Moses the list of laws at Sinai?

Paul said it in Galatians 3:24. "The Law has become our tutor to lead us to Christ, so that we may be justified by faith." The apostle explained with a personal example in Romans 7:7–11. The Law's purpose is to reveal sin. It does so by giving sin the character of a violation.

For Paul, the problem was coveting. He didn't feel the sinfulness of coveting until the Law told him, "Thou shalt not covet." But he also discovered that the Law gave him no power to obey God. He found himself coveting worse than ever. The Law acts like an X ray or CAT scan. It can reveal the tumors of sin, but it is powerless to heal them.

In other words, the Law doesn't exist to make us better, but to show us what's wrong with us and how helpless we are so we will run to Christ. Paul called the Law our "tutor." Your teachers may have helped prepare you to face life, but they don't follow you around every day telling you what to do as if you're still in kindergarten.

The Law is the speed-limit sign on the highway. It won't slow you down, but its presence gives the police officer the authority to stop you and write you a ticket. If there were no sign and the officer pulled you over for violating the speed limit, you might have a case. But once the sign reveals the law, it also reveals your sin when you fail to meet the standard.

The Law also arouses sin, as we said above (see Romans 7:8). When an unbeliever's sin nature comes face-to-face with God's requirements, it rebels and wants to do the very thing God says not to do. And the more of God's truth an unbeliever knows, the more the sin nature rebels, because it doesn't want the truth.

Again, by arousing the sinful nature we had before we came to Christ, the Law showed us just how much we needed Christ. But guess what? The Law serves the same function for us now that we know Christ. Our old nature may be dead in Christ, but our new nature is still encased in a sin-ravaged body called the flesh. And our flesh still wants to rebel against God.

So don't be confused about the Law. It's the mirror that shows us how bad we look without Christ. But you don't use your mirror to comb your hair, brush your teeth, or shave.

Legalism is the spiritual equivalent of expecting your mirror to make you beautiful. The Law of God reveals His good and perfect standard and shows us how messed up we are, but the Law can't fix what it reveals.

THE CONSEQUENCES OF LEGALISM

Did you ever wonder why a funeral procession is permitted to break the traffic laws? You've seen these processions. It doesn't matter whether there's a stop sign or a red light; the procession goes right on through. A red light means stop to you and me, but not to a funeral procession. Why? Because when a person is dead, the law no longer applies.

When you came to Jesus Christ, you died to the Law so that it no longer has any authority over you. But the legalist who casts aside that freedom and puts himself back under the Law suffers the consequences.

What are these consequences? Paul explains them in Galatians 5:

> It was for freedom that Christ set us free; therefore keep standing firm and do not be subject again to a yoke of slavery. Behold I, Paul, say to you that if you receive circumcision, Christ will be of no benefit to you. And I testify again to every man who receives circumcision, that he is under obligation to keep the whole Law. You have been severed from Christ, you who are seeking to be justified by law; you have fallen from grace. (vv. 1–4)

The believers in Galatia were being pressured to submit to circumcision as a symbol of their submission to the Mosaic Law. But there was a lot more to it than receiving a physical sign. Legalism puts people under an impossible load. Who could possibly keep the whole Law? One consequence of legalism is the joyless bondage of trying harder, yet continually falling short.

Another consequence is even more serious. What does it mean to be "severed from Christ" and "fallen from grace"? These are two ways of saying the same thing. Legalism cuts us off from the flow of God's grace.

When I preach at our church on Sunday, the congregation can see and hear me because there are all kinds of conduits and wires running through the building that supply power to the lights and the sound system. We have fine systems, but if the connection is broken everything will go dark and quiet. The equipment may be fine, but the connection is no longer intact.

Legalism cuts the connection that transmits the power and grace of God to us. When we cease operating by the grace standard and start operating by the law standard, our connection to grace is severed. This is not referring to a loss of salvation but to a loss of the enjoyment of our freedom and identity in Christ.

How do you know when this is your situation? There are several clues, some of which we mentioned earlier. You have no joy in serving Christ. Prayer is a monologue, not a dialogue—just words that fall back from the ceiling. Duty replaces delight. Everything is a chore you have to do.

It's no coincidence that the way cult leaders control their people is by putting them in bondage to their list of do's and don'ts. Pretty soon the followers are so dependent on the leader that they're incapable of relating to God or anyone else on their own.

You see, legalists have the same problem as those who are trying to work their way to heaven. That is, legalists never know when they've done enough to earn God's favor. Their list of rules to obey is never long enough. They have to keep adding to it to keep up with the demands.

If you're getting the idea that legalism is a lot of hard and frustrating work that doesn't get you anywhere, you're right. In fact, it takes you backward in your relationship with God. Legalism is not a way to please God; it's a problem that needs to be corrected.

THE CORRECTION FOR LEGALISM

Simply stated, the way to correct legalism is to maintain a relationship with God based on grace and not based on rules. Grace is what God does for us from the inside out. That's easy to say but not so easy to do. So let's look at this more closely.

Before we go any further, let me emphasize again that a relationship based on grace does not mean the absence of any rules. It means the rules grow out of the relationship, rather than being the basis of the relationship. It is love, not law, that sustains a godly life (see John 14:15; 1 John 5:3).

Sit Down with Jesus

Think of Martha and Mary that day when Jesus visited their house for dinner (Luke 10:38–42). Martha was performance-oriented, and Mary relationship-oriented. Jesus told Martha, "Mary has chosen the good part, which shall not be taken away from her" (v. 42).

Did you hear what Jesus said? Do you want the good part of your relationship with Him? Then sit at His feet and listen to Him, and let the other things find their own level. Of course, Mary would have gotten up and given Jesus a drink of water if He had asked for it. But for her, the joy of His presence was what mattered, not the menu.

The Joy of Being Free

It is so freeing to realize that we don't have to perform to please God. Once we grasp this, we don't have to let people put us under bondage anymore. Some of us are so dependent on people affirming us and complimenting us for our performance that we don't know how to live any other way.

When God saved you, He wrote His Law in your heart and mind (Hebrews 10:16). That means He wants to relate to you from the inside. You don't need an external system of rules to keep you "in line," because you have internalized God's Word and you have a desire to obey and please Him from your heart.

We can see the difference between relationship and performance in the Garden of Eden. When Adam and Eve chose the Tree of the Knowledge of Good and Evil, they chose a performance standard over their relationship with God, and they failed. But the Tree of Life was a relational tree. That tree gave life.

Throw Away Your List

Let's look at one other Scripture in closing. Paul wrote, "Not that we are adequate in ourselves to consider anything as coming from ourselves, but our adequacy is from God, who also made us adequate as servants of a new covenant, not of the letter but of the Spirit; for the letter kills, but the Spirit gives life" (2 Corinthians 3:5–6).

The word "letter" stands for the Law of Moses. It kills for the reasons we have seen. The Law only tells me how far short of the standard I have fallen, and it pronounces my judgment. When the sin within me encounters the Law, it rebels against it—and rebels deserve death in God's economy. You'll shrivel up trying to live by legalism.

Paul went on in 2 Corinthians 3:7–13 to explain that when Moses came down from Mount Sinai with the Law, his face glowed with God's glory. But the glory faded, so Moses hid his face behind a veil. That's the glory of the Law. It faded away because it was temporary.

But the new covenant of God's grace isn't like that. The glory we have is permanent, because it comes from within. The Bible says, "Now the Lord is the Spirit, and where the Spirit of the Lord is, there is liberty. But we all, with unveiled face, beholding as in a mirror the glory of the Lord, are being transformed into the same image from glory to glory, just as from the Lord, the Spirit" (2 Corinthians 3:17–18).

In the new covenant, Christ comes to live within us and brings us His unfading glory. If we will keep our eyes on Christ, His glory will rub off on us and produce glory within us. Have you ever seen someone walking a dog on a leash when the dog doesn't want to go where its owner is going? The owner is constantly tugging on the leash, pulling the dog back from here and there and telling it to stop that and come on.

That's the way a lot of Christians live. They're on a "law leash." Their lives consist of "Stop that; come back here; don't do that," only it's in terms of "Read your Bible; pray; go to church; witness." There is nothing wrong with those things, but God never meant us to do them at the end of a leash.

What a difference when you see a dog and its owner that have a strong relationship. That dog doesn't need a leash to go for a walk. Its owner can just speak a word and the dog responds. I'm not comparing Christians to dogs, but comparing performance to relationship.

Let me change the analogy. Suppose you are driving in a strange town, trying to find an address. You stop and ask for directions, and you get a complicated set of instructions that will require you to try to drive while counting stoplights and looking for street names and all of that. That's living by the law. The person giving you directions gave you the rules, so to speak, but you have to work it all out for yourself.

But suppose that person offers to drive you to your destination.

Now everything is different. You can throw your list of rules out the window because someone who knows the way is in control. You can sit back and enjoy the ride.

Too many Christians are trying to follow a list of rules to get them where they want to go. Their destination is peace and joy and victory, but they really don't know how to get there. If this is your situation, Jesus Christ is inviting you to move over and let Him have the wheel because He can take you where you want to go. (And, by the way, throw your list out the window on the trip!)

Chapter Seven

THE MARVEL OF GRACE

One day a man who didn't have much money was given what he considered the gift of a lifetime. He had always wanted to go on a cruise, but he knew he could never afford it. However, a kind friend knew of the man's desire and gave him a ticket to a luxurious seven-day cruise.

The man was overjoyed, but he was worried that he wouldn't be able to afford the lavish meals on the cruise ship. So he made himself a week's worth of peanut butter and jelly sandwiches and headed off for his cruise.

At every meal, the man walked by the beautiful buffets and elaborate meals prepared by the ship's crew. Then he would sigh, go back to his cabin, and eat his peanut butter and jelly sandwich.

But after a few days of this, he couldn't stand it any longer. So one evening he asked a steward, "How much do I need to pay to eat this meal?"

The steward looked at him in surprise and said, "Sir, don't you know that the meals come with your ticket? You don't have to pay anything. Eat all you want."

The man didn't understand that his friend's gift was a package deal. His ticket entitled him to everything the cruise ship had to offer. A lot of Christians today are like that badly informed cruise ship passenger. They're eating peanut butter and jelly sandwiches when they could have a feast, because they don't understand the true nature of God's grace. Your discovery of who you are in Christ will take a giant leap forward when you fully understand grace and what it means in your life.

THE GIFT OF GRACE

The first thing I want us to see is the gift of grace. But first, here is a basic definition of the biblical term *grace.* Grace is God's unmerited favor poured out on the undeserving.

I like to define grace as the inexhaustible supply of God's goodness, doing for us what we do not deserve, could never earn, and could never repay. Grace is all that God is free to do for us based on the work of Christ.

Understanding how grace works can be powerful in helping to set you free for the reason suggested above. Grace is a *gift,* and as such the key to it is not what you do for God but what He does for you. The best thing you can do with a gift is to receive it with gratitude. Let me give you several distinguishing characteristics of God's gift called grace.

Grace Is Opposed to Works

There are a lot of Bible verses you ought to memorize and carry around in your head. Here's one of them. Speaking of the remnant of Israel that believes in Christ, Paul said, "But if [this remnant] is by grace, it is no longer on the basis of works, otherwise grace is no longer grace" (Romans 11:6).

What is true of God's work with Israel is true of God's work with us. Human works, our own efforts to make ourselves acceptable to God, are so antithetical to grace that the two cancel each other out. Paul told the Galatians, "I do not nullify the grace of God, for if righteousness comes through the Law, then Christ died needlessly" (2:21).

The Law demands human works, as we have already seen. But Christ had to die because we could never work our way to heaven. There is no room for works in God's salvation. He has zero tolerance for mixing grace with law, because works insult His Son's work on the cross.

Human works as epitomized in trying to keep the Law are not only counter to grace, they are counterproductive to grace. Remember what we learned earlier. Sin finds its power in the Law (see 1 Corinthians 15:56). Even though the Law isn't sinful, we are—so when our sinful flesh runs up against God's law, the flesh immediately wants to rebel and sin.

If you are a performance-based Christian—a legalist—you won't appreciate grace. In fact, your performance will cancel the very grace you pray for. A lot of Christians don't realize that after they get on their knees and ask God to help them, they get up off their knees and cancel that request by gritting their teeth and trying to perform to win God's approval.

Grace Is Free

We said above that grace is free. Not cheap by any means, but free (see Revelation 22:17). The Bible says we are justified "as a gift by [God's] grace" (Romans 3:24).

This truth finds its classic statement in Ephesians 2:8–9. "For by grace you have been saved through faith; and that not of yourselves, it is the gift of God; not as a result of works, so that no one may boast."

Free means no charge at all, no strings attached. Suppose I invite you to dinner and we have a great evening, but when you get ready to go home I surprise you with a bill of fifty dollars for the meal. Our relationship would change drastically, from one of grace to one of obligation. The meal would no longer be a gift of grace, but merely a service for which I charge you a fee.

A lot of modern marketing cleverly mixes works and grace. For instance, the "Buy one, get one free" ad isn't really a free offer. If it were, the ad would simply say, "Get one free." What makes grace so marvelous is that it is absolutely free.

Grace Is All-Inclusive

Grace is also an all-inclusive offer, as we suggested in the story at the beginning of the chapter. The Bible says, "Blessed be the God and Father of our Lord Jesus Christ, who has blessed us with every spiritual blessing in the heavenly places in Christ" (Ephesians 1:3). Everything you will ever need, God has already provided in the grace He has displayed to us in Christ.

Grace is risky business.

As we said in the previous chapter, too many Christians accept Christ as Savior by grace, but then seek to live the Christian life by the works of the Law. That's because they're confused about grace.

It's important to realize that the grace that saves us is not static. Peter tells us, "Grow in the grace and knowledge of our Lord and Savior Jesus Christ" (2 Peter 3:18). Grace not only saves you for heaven, but grace equips you for a life of spiritual growth and maturity here on earth.

Don't worry about having to find some spiritual experience that will take you higher or deeper than the grace that saves you. God doesn't have anything higher or deeper than His grace. We just need to discover how high and deep it is.

You can buy any of several levels of cars. You can purchase the basic package that doesn't have much except the essentials. Or you can buy an options package that has a few of the features that make driving a little more enjoyable, like power windows, air-conditioning, and cruise control.

Then there is the car that has it all—the complete package, right down to the gold lettering. No detail for your benefit is left out. Guess which package God purchased for you when He gave His Son on the cross? All the options are included in grace.

But anytime you offer something valuable free of charge, there is a risk attached. Grace is risky business.

Grace Is Risky

As Paul explained God's grace to the church at Rome, he understood that some of his readers might wonder if grace was really all that marvelous, while others might try to abuse grace. So he wrote, "The Law came in so that the transgression would increase; but where sin increased, grace abounded all the more" (Romans 5:20). The law of God shows us that we're far more sinful than we ever thought we were. But once we realize how bad off we are, and how far God's grace reaches beyond the extent of our sin, we won't have any doubts about the marvel of grace.

Paul also had a word for those who figured that the abounding nature of grace meant they could sin all they want and then run to God for forgiveness. Their twisted argument was that sin was good because more sin released more grace. Some people have taken that approach to the Christian life, in their actions if not in their words.

The risk of grace is that some will try to take advantage of God's goodness. But God is willing to take that risk. His grace is so marvelous that God will give it to us and endure the pain of our misusing it. God is willing to take the risk of saving us freely and then having us forget how great the gift of salvation is (see 2 Peter 1:9).

Some believers who are unwilling to accept the risks of grace have adopted a theology of salvation that includes works as part of the gospel message. But grace involves the "risk" that we can be justified before God and accepted by Him solely on the basis of what Christ has done, not what we can do.

Do you know how I know that grace could only come from God alone? Because if most of us gave something very precious to people and they began abusing it or forgot to say thanks, we would stop giving and say, "That's it. No more gifts." Thank God that He doesn't do that with us.

THE GREATNESS OF GRACE

Grace is not only a gift, it is a *great* gift. Paul almost ran out of superlatives describing grace on one occasion. "God is able to make all grace abound to you, so that always having all sufficiency in everything, you may have an abundance for every good deed" (2 Corinthians 9:8).

Always an Abundance

This was written in relation to our giving to God's work, the principle being that we can never outgive God. That's true in every area because His grace is so great it reaches beyond anything we can measure. We have a supply of grace to cover anything we can face and leave us with an abundance.

You know you are living in grace when there is an abundance. You don't just have joy, but "joy inexpressible and full of glory" (1 Peter 1:8). Not just peace, but "peace . . . which surpasses all comprehension" (Philippians 4:7).

Paul knew about the abundance of grace for any circumstance. Paul had a terrible trial that was like "a thorn in the flesh" to him (2 Corinthians 12:7). It burdened him so much that he pleaded three times for God remove it. But His answer was, "My grace is sufficient for you, for power is perfected in weakness" (v. 9).

Paul responded, in so many words, "Thank You, Lord! Your grace is enough for me, because it makes me the strongest when I'm the weakest" (see v. 10). Grace gave Paul an abundance even when he had nothing left within himself.

A Great Teacher

God's grace is also great because of what it teaches us. For this we turn to Paul, the apostle of grace, once again: "For the grace of God has appeared, bringing salvation to all men, instructing us to deny ungodliness and worldly desires and to live sensibly, righteously and godly in the present age" (Titus 2:11–12). Grace not only teaches us how to get to heaven someday but how to bring heaven down to earth today.

If you really know your Bible, you might be saying at this point, "Wait a minute, Tony. Doesn't Paul say somewhere that the Law is our teacher to bring us to Christ?"

Paul did tell the Galatians, "The Law has become our tutor to lead us to Christ, that we may be justified by faith" (3:24). But the word *tutor* here really refers to someone who was more of a custodian than a teacher—someone like a child-care worker who makes sure a child gets on the school bus.

The only thing the Law could do was get us on the bus and drive us to Christ. We've discussed the problem with the Law, which is that it could only tell us what to do or not to do, without giving us the power to obey.

Law will give you information, but not ability. Law will give you the doctrine, but it doesn't enable the duty. Law will give you the facts, but it won't enable you to function. Grace, however, not only teaches us what to do but grants us the power to do it.

Grace teaches us to say no to what is wrong and yes to what is right, and then it says, "Here is the ability to obey." The Law says, "Thou shalt not lie," but grace comes alongside and enables you to put aside lying and live in the truth.

This principle of grace is all around us. Why haven't all the fish in all of the world's seas and oceans and rivers exhausted their supply of water in which to swim? Because a gracious God gives them more water than they will ever need. Why don't the animals in the forest run out of foliage, or human beings run out of air to breathe? Because God's grace keeps on giving.

But notice something else. God's grace is so great that He doesn't simply give fish water to swim in, but gills to filter it. He not only gives us oxygen, but lungs to use it. Grace not only gives you what you need, but an abundance for every need and the ability to use the gift properly.

GETTING THE GIFT OF GRACE

Since grace is such a great gift, we need to know how to get our hands on it. I'm speaking to Christians who have been saved by grace, but who may not know how to make the grace that saved them a reality in their daily walk with Christ.

Learning to Abide

Jesus gave us the key to putting grace to work when He said, "Abide in Me, and I in you. As the branch cannot bear fruit of itself unless it abides in the vine, so neither can you unless you abide in Me. . . . For apart from Me you can do nothing" (John 15:4–5).

We can learn a lot from the way fruit grows. I've never heard a grape grunting and groaning to be "grapey." All a grape does is abide in the vine, and the vine produces what the grape needs. The grape's connection with its source is what produces its fruitfulness.

Abiding is a word we don't hear very often these days, but people use another word that has the same basic meaning: *bonding*. People talk about bonding with another person, forming a connection that brings the two people together in a vital, even life-changing, relationship.

That's the kind of relationship Jesus wants us to have with Him, so that we can produce the fruit that His grace wants to produce in us.

The Gift That Keeps on Giving

We get the gift of grace for each day the same way we got the gift of grace for our salvation: by receiving it freely from Christ. That's why the Bible tells us, "Therefore as you have received Christ Jesus the Lord, so walk in Him" (Colossians 2:6). The Christian life is a grace adventure from first to last.

When you receive the gift of grace for daily Christian living, you no longer just pray, "Lord, I don't want to tell a lie today," but, "Lord, I give You the freedom to express Your truth through me."

Grace gets you beyond just praying, "Lord, I'm going to try not to yield to lust today." Instead, you're able to pray, "Lord, by Your grace I allow You to express Your purity of mind through me today."

When you start living like this, really living by grace, you wind up doing things you never thought you could do before. You wind up loving folk you couldn't stand before. You wind up being able to control things in your life you couldn't control before.

The key to grace living is not more self-effort and trying harder but getting closer to Christ. That's where the power is, as Paul knew so well. His passion in life was "that I may know [Christ] and the power of His resurrection" (Philippians 3:10).

Power That Never Runs Low

I mentioned earlier that I'm starting to learn how to use a computer. I've already learned one basic fact, which is that there are two ways to power a computer. You can run it on a battery, which of course runs down and needs recharging, or you can plug your computer into an ever-flowing power source.

The problem with the battery is that if you forget to recharge it, or can't get to a power source to recharge it, your computer will eventually stop working.

Too many Christians are running by battery power instead of God's ever-flowing grace. They come to church on Sunday to get spiritually recharged, but they begin to run out of power, so they have to come on Wednesday night for a midweek recharge. If they miss a week, watch out, because their spiritual battery is dangerously low.

But when you plug that computer into a permanent power source, an abiding takes place. The power never runs low because there is a connectedness between the computer and its power source that becomes a way of life.

Working Out What God Works In

Just in case you're beginning to think that the life of grace sounds pretty passive, with nothing for us to do, we need to look at two crucial verses that clarify the relationship between the good works God wants us to do and the grace we need to do them: "So then, my beloved, just as you have always obeyed, not as in my presence only, but now much more in my absence, work out your salvation with fear and trembling; for it is God who is at work in you, both to will and to work for His good pleasure" (Philippians 2:12–13).

This is a passage you need to read all the way through, because if you quit at verse 12 you may get the idea that the Christian life depends on what you do. But the only reason we can work out our salvation is that God is working within us. In terms of our lives, verse 13 actually comes before verse 12, since the key to this is what God is doing in grace. Everything we do is simply an expression of His work.

Works and grace are mutually exclusive when it comes to salvation, but they have an important relationship in a Christian's life. When grace is at work, the works we do for the Lord are inspired and enabled by grace. It's not that we're working to gain God's favor, but we're working out what He has already worked in.

To put it another way, both the Old and the New Testament command us not to lie (Exodus 20:16; Colossians 3:9). The difference is that the Law states it as a command, period. The command is just as strong under grace, because God's standards do not change. But because we are operating under grace, God's commands become an opportunity to display the character of Christ through us as we draw on the power of God working within us. This is how we activate the gift of grace for daily living.

THE GIVER OF GRACE

Gifts don't just materialize out of nowhere. A gift requires a giver, and there is only one Giver great enough to give us a gift as wonderful as grace.

Jesus Christ said He came to give us abundant life (see John 10:10), a life that includes His grace. Jesus alone is able to give us grace because "grace and truth were realized through Jesus Christ" (John 1:17). Christ is the One through whom God's grace has been manifested on this earth, and we can reflect this grace in our lives because we belong to Christ.

In fact, John said just before this that we have received "grace upon grace" from Christ (v. 16). In other words, we have received "super grace." The secret to this "super grace" is allowing Christ to live out His perfect, sinless life through us in the power of His resurrection. The fact is that we are saved by Christ's sinless life as well as by His death, a concept we explained in detail in chapter 5 (which you may want to review). Suffice it to say that the goal of the Christian life is "that the life of Jesus . . . may be manifested in our mortal flesh" (2 Corinthians 4:11).

The combination of Christ's righteousness and resurrection power at work in you is more than enough to put grace to work in your life. With all that power and perfection at work within you, your job is to cooperate with rather than resist the workings of God in grace.

I like to compare God's grace working within us to the job a respirator does for someone who is unable to breathe on his own. As long as the patient can breathe on his own power, the respirator does him no good. But when the patient cooperates with the respirator, things happen. The patient is still involved in the process, since the oxygen is going into and out of his mouth and lungs. The patient and the respirator are working in unison, but the machine is doing the work. Unfortunately, too many Christians are still hyperventilating trying to do something for God.

Jesus Christ wants to express His life through you and be your respirator. You can't breathe spiritually without Him, and neither can I. His grace is the very oxygen in our lungs that makes the spiritual life possible. As we yield ourselves to Christ, He fills us with the incredible, life-giving gift of grace.

Chapter Eight

WALKING BY THE FLESH

One of the most popular sitcoms on television twenty years ago was a program called *Diff'rent Strokes.* The show revolved around Arnold and Willis, two boys whose mother was the maid for a wealthy man named Mr. Drummond.

The boys' mother died, so Mr. Drummond adopted them and made them his sons rather than let them drift back into the government projects out of which they had come. Most of the show's comedy involved the boys' attempts to learn how to live in the penthouse instead of the projects.

This TV family discovered that while it was one thing to get these boys out of the projects, it was another thing altogether to get the projects out of them. They were in a new environment, but they often had a hard time adjusting to their new environment because it's hard to get rid of old behavior patterns once they have become established.

You know where I'm going with this. When God found you and me, we were in the spiritual projects. We were lost, but He saved us and brought us into His spiritual penthouse, the heavenly places in Christ Jesus. However, even though we are new people, we brought along with us the thinking and behavior patterns from the old neighborhood.

We know by now that God calls those old sinful patterns operating in the body the "flesh," what theologians refer to as our unredeemed humanity. The question before us as believers is this: Now that we have been adopted by our glorious new Father and have a totally new identity, how do we learn to live in our new environment and enjoy all of its privileges and benefits, rather than allowing the old patterns of thinking and acting to control us?

The difference between living by our old identity in Adam or our new identity in Christ is the difference between walking by the flesh or walking by the Spirit. This is the dichotomy the Bible sets up, and these are the terms Scripture uses to describe two patterns of life we can follow as Christians.

According to Paul, when it comes to our identity we are those "who do not walk according to the flesh but according to the Spirit" (Romans 8:4). We're going to see, however, that it is still possible for Christians to be dominated by the flesh.

This is a two-sided coin, so we are going to spend the next two chapters talking about the difference between a flesh-dominated life and a Spirit-directed life. I want to start with the negative, what the Bible calls walking by the flesh, so we can deal with those old patterns and get them out of the way in preparation to learning how to walk by the Spirit.

A DEFINITION OF THE FLESH

Let's start with a definition of walking by the flesh. Actually, we stated it earlier. This is a way of life patterned after the thoughts, habits, and desires of our sin-contaminated flesh that we brought with us into our new life with Christ.

We read above that Paul used the physical activity of walking to illustrate the spiritual reality of living according to the flesh or the Spirit.

Walking by the Flesh

Walking is a good analogy because it involves several factors. First, walking involves *dependence.* I must depend on my feet and legs to support my weight as I put one foot in front of the other. If you have ever badly twisted your ankle or knee and then tried to put your weight on it, you realize very quickly how dependent you are on your legs and feet to walk.

Walking also involves a *destination*. You can walk in place if you want to, but generally if you are walking you have a goal in mind, even if it's just to get to the other side of the room. Walking is a purposeful activity.

Finally, walking also involves *dedication*. You haven't really walked if you just take a step or two today and quit, then try another step or two tomorrow. Walking requires us to keep on putting one foot in front of the other.

Most of us don't think in terms of these factors when we walk, because we have been walking for so long we're used to it. We just get up and walk without giving it a second thought. Can you see why walking is a good analogy for living? Most of us live the way we walk—unconsciously, by habit. We learned to walk years ago, and we do it without thinking.

A Pattern of Self-Sufficiency

So it is with the patterns of our flesh. The way we lived before we met Christ has become so ingrained that we follow the flesh without even thinking. To walk by the flesh, then, is to depend upon yourself to take you where you want to go, to be dedicated to meeting the needs of your flesh, and to set out with the destination or goal in mind of meeting those needs in a self-centered way.

I added this last part because self-sufficiency is simply a synonym for the flesh. This is important because when we have an "I can do it myself" attitude, we contradict Jesus who said, "Apart from Me you can do nothing" (John 15:5). And when you begin contradicting Jesus, God begins to resist your efforts (see James 4:6).

Trying to Help God

The problem with walking by the flesh isn't simply that the flesh leads us into evil. The flesh can also get religious and try to help God out. Abraham and Sarah are a great illustration of this during the years they waited for God to fulfill His promise and give them a child.

God had told Abraham, "One who will come forth from your own body, he shall be your heir" (Genesis 15:4). But Sarah was ninety years old and had never been able to have a child. Old Abe wasn't getting any younger, either.

So when Sarah decided that God must not know how old they were and how slim their chances of having a child were, she came up with a plan to help God's promise along. Abraham agreed to the plan, which you can read about in Genesis 16. He took Hagar, Sarah's obviously much younger servant, as his second wife.

Hagar became pregnant just as they planned, and she gave birth to Ishmael. Ishmael was Abraham's offspring, but there was just one problem. The Bible says that from God's standpoint, Ishmael was born "according to the flesh," whereas Isaac was born later "through the promise" (Galatians 4:23).

That phrase "according to the flesh" means trouble. Ishmael was a son of the flesh because his birth was a human attempt to help God carry out His plan.

So God rejected Ishmael in terms of His promise because Ishmael was the product of self-sufficient human beings trying to assist God. The motives of Abraham and Sarah were good. But please take note that even when you use the flesh to try to do something good, God rejects it.

The Flesh Doesn't Count

Paul said that *nothing* good dwells in our sin-contaminated flesh (Romans 7:18). The problem is that most of us don't really believe that, and we prove it every time we walk by the flesh.

After Abraham had tried it his way, God came and restated His promise of a son. From then on, Abraham did not waver in his faith.

When he learned to live in terms of the Spirit and not the flesh, Isaac, the son of promise, was born.

Before we leave Abraham, let me show you something else interesting. When God commanded Abraham to sacrifice Isaac, His instruction was, "Take now your son, your only son" (Genesis 22:2).

Why did God say that, knowing that Abraham had another son named Ishmael? Because of what we said earlier. Ishmael didn't count because he was a product of the flesh. Anything you do out of self-sufficiency doesn't count with God. The birth of Ishmael was natural, whereas the birth of Isaac was supernatural.

God did care about Ishmael, so don't misunderstand. But the point is still made that fleshly activity doesn't carry any weight with Him. Some of us have been doing things for years, even things for God, that don't count because we've been doing them in the energy of our flesh.

Programmed for Failure

We need to understand that our flesh has been programmed to do what it does by things such as years of sinful actions, performance, and fulfilling the expectations of others.

For some of us, our flesh was programmed by our parents because we grew up with a performance-based relationship. In order to win our parents' approval, we had to do this or that.

Others of us have learned to please our flesh by feeding it on sinful habits such as drugs, pornography, greed, or whatever our particular vice might be. These things then become the primary way we experience pleasure.

Still others of us have fulfilled our need for acceptance and self-esteem by performing for and trying to please people. We have developed a "performance habit" to win friends and influence people.

But it doesn't matter whether we are talking about the rankest sin or a socially acceptable behavior, it's all a matter of walking by the flesh—and it's a program destined for failure.

THE DESIRE OF THE FLESH

Now that we know something of what the flesh is all about, let's find out what the flesh wants to do with us. What is the desire of the flesh?

Seeking Your Destruction

We can answer that very succinctly. Paul wrote, "The mind set on the flesh is death" (Romans 8:6). What does the flesh want to do with you? It wants to kill you. It wants to hook your mind and lead you to death.

This does not necessarily mean that every person who walks by the flesh is going to collapse. Some people have been walking by the flesh for years and they're still around.

The answer, of course, is that death in the Bible is a spiritual as well as a physical reality. Sinners are dead in their trespasses and sins (Ephesians 2:1) even while they are physically alive. Death can mean the absence or the cessation of spiritual function.

So what the flesh wants to do is kill the operation of the Holy Spirit working within us. This is exactly the opposite of what the Spirit wants to do, because Paul went on to say in Romans 8:6, "But the mind set on the Spirit is life and peace."

Passages like this may sound like they can't be written to Christians. But only Christians have the choice of walking in the flesh or walking in the Spirit. Non-Christians are living in the flesh, period.

When we allow our minds to be set on the flesh, we are robbed of the abundant life Jesus came to give us. The flesh is like the defensive unit of a football team, whose only goal is to kill the offensive team's progress and force it off the field.

In fact, football commentators will often say that a penalty or a great play by the defense "killed" an offensive team's drive toward the goal line. That's what the devil wants to do to us by getting us to walk by the flesh. The defense doesn't want the offense to get anywhere within scoring range.

A Picture of the Flesh

How do you know when you are walking by the flesh? What are the signs? Well, you may be walking by the flesh if you are living on a spiritual roller coaster, up and down all the time.

You may be walking by the flesh if you are burned out from performing for other people or even for God. You may be walking by the flesh if your spiritual battery that you got all charged up on Sunday is drained by Tuesday.

Here are two more possibilities: You may be walking by the flesh if you spend most of your time judging how other people are doing. And you are most definitely walking by the flesh if there is nothing supernatural about your life—nothing happening with you that can't be explained except by the power of God at work.

The flesh wants to post a big, fat zero on the scoreboard of your spiritual life.

We really don't have to guess at what a person who is walking by the flesh looks like, because God's Word gives us a clear picture in Galatians 5:19–21. If you want to know whether you are being controlled by the flesh, look at these three categories.

First, look at your morality. "Now the deeds of the flesh are evident, which are: immorality, impurity, sensuality . . . drunkenness, carousing" (Galatians 5:19, 21a).

Second, check out your religion. The list of fleshly activities continues in verse 20 with "idolatry [and] sorcery." Remember we said that the flesh likes to act religious, even if it's false religion.

Third, examine your relationships. Instead of life and peace, the flesh produces "enmities, strife, jealousy, outbursts of anger, disputes, dissensions, factions, envying" (vv. 20–21a).

That's quite a list, and it's not even a full portrait of the flesh. Paul said there were other "things like these" that he didn't take time to mention (v. 21).

A Big, Fat Zero

The flesh knows you want to grow in Christ, and it is determined to stop you at all costs. Going back to our football analogy, when was the last time you heard of a defense feeling sorry for the other team and letting those players score just one touchdown so they won't be so discouraged?

Not a chance. A good defense wants to shut the other team out. In the same way, the flesh wants to post a big, fat zero on the scoreboard of your spiritual life.

You may say, "Well, since the flesh is this determined to stop me, I'll just try harder to walk by the Spirit." And you start making all kinds of promises to yourself and to God.

We've said it more than once. Trying harder is not the way to find freedom and power in the Christian life. In fact, I need to tell you something. The flesh *loves* it when you make promises to try harder and do better, because that means you are relying on your flesh to help you defeat your flesh.

Bad idea! That's like a football team on offense inviting the captain of the defensive team into its huddle. What's going to happen? The defender is going to hear the play, then run back to his side with a big smile on his face and inform his teammates of your play so they can crush you. Don't expect any help from the flesh in living for Christ, because the flesh's desire is to kill any spiritual progress on your part.

THE DECEPTION OF THE FLESH

You have probably figured out by now that the flesh is very deceptive. It doesn't always hit you between the eyes with something obviously sinful. The flesh likes to sneak up and blindside you.

Paul was waylaid by the flesh. He described the problem in Romans 7:7–12, which we have already studied in detail. I would just point out verse 11 again, where the apostle said that sin, or the flesh, took advantage of the perfect standard of God's Law to deceive and kill him.

No wonder Paul said the Galatian believers had been "bewitched" by those who were trying to put them back under the Law (3:1).

The flesh wants to deceive you into thinking that you can be good and sincere and determined enough to do what God wants you to do. The flesh wants you to fixate on the Law, because when you do that you are sowing the seeds of your own spiritual defeat.

No Debt to the Flesh

Another deception of the flesh is that you have an obligation to walk by the flesh, but the fact is that you owe your flesh nothing. Paul made that very clear. "So then, brethren, we are under obligation, not to the flesh, to live according to the flesh" (Romans 8:12).

You see, you can't afford to obligate yourself to the flesh because once you do that, the flesh will never let you forget the debt. That's what addiction is all about.

An addiction, whether physical or emotional or sexual or any other kind, is a craving of the flesh. It's your flesh saying, "You need me. You'll never make it without me. You'll never be able to shake me." That's a lie, a deception, but it's amazing how many people believe it.

Before we talk about how to defeat the flesh, let me point out something else that is really crucial to this issue of the flesh. We could state it this way: Not all flesh is equal. Let me show you what I mean.

It's All Bad

We know that people don't all act the same. Some people's flesh manifests itself in evil deeds, while others perform good deeds. We might call these "bad flesh" and "good flesh" people.

Before he met Jesus, Paul was definitely in the latter category. In fact, he had "super flesh." Paul himself said, "If anyone else has a mind to put confidence in the flesh, I far more" (Philippians 3:4). In other words, if good flesh could get the job done spiritually, Paul would have had it made before God. He had a pedigree few others could match (vv. 5–6).

Paul was saying that if we are going to grade people by fleshly standards, he would have been grade A prime. People like this are often the hardest to reach for Christ because they don't see why they need a Savior. They are confident of heaven because they're so good, especially compared to everyone else. That's why the Bible warns against the danger of measuring ourselves by each other (2 Corinthians 10:12).

Just before talking about his fleshly accomplishments, Paul gave us the real deal. "We are the true circumcision, who worship in the Spirit of God and glory in Christ Jesus and put no confidence in the flesh" (Philippians 3:3).

Paul knew better than to trust his flesh, because all flesh is bad in God's sight. So he told the Philippians, "Whatever things were gain to me, those things I have counted as loss for the sake of Christ" (3:7). In fact, when he thought himself so righteous, he was actively working against God by persecuting Christ's church.

HOW TO DEFEAT THE FLESH

Since the flesh—this sin-contaminated container in which our new nature must temporarily live—is irredeemable and deceptive and out to trip us up, we need a spiritual game plan that will allow us to defeat the flesh.

A Winning Game Plan

We'll talk about this in detail in the next chapter as we discuss walking by the Spirit. Let me just give you a little glimpse into the process as we close this part of our study.

In the last two verses of Romans 7 and the beginning of chapter 8, Paul gave us a winning game plan for defeating the flesh. The apostle needed a plan, because his battle with the flesh had left him crying out, "Wretched man that I am! Who will set me free from the body of this death?" (Romans 7:24).

Paul needed freedom from the flesh that was keeping him from being free at last and enjoying his spiritual freedom through his identity with Christ. The key to victory lay in the difference between the activity of Paul's mind and his flesh. "On the one hand I myself with my mind am serving the law of God, but on the other, with my flesh the law of sin" (v. 25).

The mind that Paul said was his real self was the new nature he received in Christ. This nature serves God because it can't do anything else. But the flesh serves sin for the same reason, because it can't do anything else.

When we put these two realities side by side, it becomes obvious that to defeat the flesh we need to learn how to live in our new nature that is perfect and can't do anything but serve God. Or in the words of Galatians 5:16, we need to learn to "walk by the Spirit." When we do that, the flesh loses its grip. Many of us have decided we're never going to get better or have victory over the things that are defeating us. Many of us view our weaknesses like we do a cold. Since there is no cure for a cold, we just do the best we can to manage the symptoms.

But that wasn't Paul's view. "The law of the Spirit of life in Christ Jesus has set you free from the law of sin and of death" (Romans 8:2). Walking by the Spirit will set us free from the flesh that dogs us.

Free at Last

The flesh is like a prison. Inmates in a prison are locked up behind bars and high walls and barbed wire. It doesn't matter how hard they beat on those bars or walls, they will not be able to break free. They are trapped.

A bird can fly into a prison yard, soar around, and even land behind the prison walls. But that bird is really free. Why? Because it is operating by a radically different principle than those prisoners. The bird can soar up and over the walls anytime it wants.

Outside of Jesus Christ, we are prisoners behind bars and walls. It doesn't matter what we do, we cannot break free of the law of sin and death and the prison of the flesh.

But when Jesus Christ saved us, He created a brand-new entity that can fly and can set us free from the confining walls of the law of sin and death. When we learn how to live by the soaring power of the Holy Spirit and Christ expresses His life through us, we're on our way to spiritual victory.

Getting Rid of "the Blob"

What many Christians need to do is change their environment—to stop living in the realm of the flesh and move into the environment of the Spirit. It reminds me of one of my favorite old movies, called *The Blob.*

In the movie this mass of cosmic gelatin fell to earth from space and began to consume people. The blob would just flow over people and envelop them, and they were gone.

The blob's first victim was an old man, and the more the man tried to shake off the blob, the more it consumed him. He was rushed to a hospital, but the doctors couldn't figure out what was wrong. They left the emergency room for a few moments, and when they came back the man had been totally consumed. In fact, the blob even consumed the doctor.

The authorities tried everything they knew to get rid of the blob, but nothing worked. But at the end of the movie, they made the discovery that the blob could not deal with cold. Whenever the blob encountered cold, it backed off. When the cold was taken away, it revived and moved forward again, but when they sprayed something cold on it, it would back up.

So the authorities froze the blob, put it in a crate, and flew the crate to Alaska. They could not destroy the blob, but when they changed its environment, the blob was rendered inactive.

When Jesus saved you, He brought you into a brand-new environment. The "blob" of your flesh can't handle this new realm. But until you understand and use your new environment, then you won't benefit from it. You'll spend all your time trying to rid yourself of the blob of your flesh.

God has prepared an environment for you that is so perfect the sinful flesh can't survive and thrive there. You enter this environment when you cease putting your confidence in the flesh and abandon your self-sufficiency and live in the power of the Holy Spirit. Let's find out more about what this life involves.

Chapter Nine

WALKING BY THE SPIRIT

On several occasions, I have boarded an airplane with my wife, Lois, and a number of our church members and listeners to our radio program for a ministry tour of Israel. These are unforgettable, life-changing experiences, made possible at least in part by the wonderful law of aerodynamics.

I'm a big fan of this law because it allows me to go places I probably would never see otherwise and minister to people I would probably never meet any other way. Aerodynamics is a great law or principle because it allows us to supersede the law of gravity.

The law of gravity simply dictates that what goes up must come down. I'm tied to the earth by this law, which pulls me down no matter how high I jump or how hard I flap my arms and try to fly. Gravity is very confining and limiting when you want to take to the skies and go to some far-off place.

But thanks to the law of aerodynamics, I can board an airplane specifically designed to take advantage of certain principles of speed and motion and airflow that lift that plane into the sky even though gravity is still pulling on it. For the duration of my flight, I enjoy the benefits from a higher law that sets me free from my human limitations.

God has put a higher law into effect for us as believers, and its benefits are not temporary. It's true that the flesh continues to exert a downward pull on us because we are living in a body of flesh ruined by sin. But it's also true that "the law of the Spirit of life in Christ Jesus has set you free from the law of sin and of death" (Romans 8:2).

Notice that for the present time, the law of the Spirit does not obliterate the flesh—although that will happen when Jesus returns. The Spirit's law supersedes the law of the flesh and renders it ineffective, in much the same way that aerodynamics allows us to escape the downward pull of the law of gravity.

Paul went on to say that this higher law is in effect for those "who do not walk according to the flesh but according to the Spirit" (Romans 8:4).

Then in verse 5 we learn that this life in the Spirit that allows us to escape the downward pull of the flesh is located and activated in our minds. As we saw in the previous chapter, Paul used the physical activity of walking to illustrate a spiritual principle. I want to make four observations about walking by the Spirit.

THE PRINCIPLE OF WALKING BY THE SPIRIT

We've touched briefly on Galatians 5, the Bible's seminal teaching on walking by the Spirit, so we need to consider this passage in detail. Paul wrote, "But I say, walk by the Spirit, and you will not carry out the desire of the flesh" (v. 16).

He then followed this with a selected list of the flesh's products and the fruit of the Spirit (vv. 17–23). We've discussed the first half of that list. In this chapter we'll deal with the fruit the Holy Spirit wants to produce in us.

Activating the Spirit's Power

That little preposition translated "by" in verse 16 is very important. It has the idea "by means of." We could paraphrase this verse,

"Live or conduct yourselves by means of the Spirit's power and enabling, as opposed to the power of the flesh, and then you will not fulfill or carry out the desire of the flesh."

That's the idea Paul was communicating. Before we break this down, notice that the verse does *not* say, "Walk by the Spirit, and you will no longer even be bothered by the desires of the flesh." Living in step with the Holy Spirit does not negate the flesh's desire to act independently of God, as we can readily verify from our own experience.

When your flesh wants to do wrong, don't be surprised, because that's what the flesh does. Those feelings are real, and no amount of spiritual hocus-pocus can make them just disappear. But when you are walking by the Spirit, you will be able to tell the flesh what to do instead of the flesh calling the shots.

The key to walking by the Spirit is what we set our minds on.

We have seen that in Romans 8, Paul contrasted living by the Spirit with living by trying to keep the Law, which is another term for living by the flesh. The reason is that any attempt at law-keeping is an activity of the flesh because it's all self-induced righteousness, which falls short of God's requirements.

Whenever you see a Christian trying to please God by obeying a list of rules, you can be pretty sure that person has not yet learned to walk by the Spirit. A Spirit-directed life renders law-keeping obsolete, because it is energized by the higher law of God's grace and our grateful response of love to that grace.

We have already talked about the law's limitations in terms of enabling us to obey. The law sets the speed limit, and the law will convict you if you break it. But the law can't help you obey. In fact, when you *do* obey, the law does not come around to encourage you. Police officers don't pull people over and congratulate them for obeying the traffic laws.

Walking by the Spirit, the life of spiritual freedom based on our new identity in Christ, is a continuous, purposeful, and committed way of life. The analogy of walking suggests a deliberate activity to reach a desired goal.

One contrast is the kind of frantic, run-till-you-drop type of Christianity that often marks those who have put their relationship with God on a performance basis. Another contrast is a passive spirituality that sits around waiting for the Spirit to move you. Neither option reflects God's desire for us.

Setting Your Mind on Things Above

According to Paul, the key to walking by the Spirit is what we set our minds on (Romans 8:5–6). This is a valuable concept because the spiritual life really begins in the mind, which encompasses your inner being or spirit where the real you lives. This is the part of you that will live forever after your body has turned back to dust and has been replaced with an indestructible body.

Obviously, then, what we do with our minds is determinative of whether we will live free in the Spirit or allow ourselves to be put back into spiritual shackles. The Bible commands us, "Set your mind on the things above, not on the things that are on earth" (Colossians 3:2). How do we set our minds on the things above, the things of the Spirit?

We do this when we think in alignment with what the Spirit thinks about us. To put it in our familiar terms, to walk by the Spirit is to think of your new identity in Christ, not your old identity in Adam.

Which is more true and more in tune with reality, what God thinks about you, or what you or anybody else thinks about you? Walking by the Spirit means operating by God's definition of who you are—and He says you are a new creation in Christ (2 Corinthians 5:17).

This gets very practical in terms of everyday life. When your flesh is saying, "I have to have this," "I want that," or "You can't get along without this," at that point you can set your mind on things above and announce to your flesh, "I am a new creature in Christ, and I don't have to have any of this stuff."

At this point your mind is in conflict with your feelings, and that can be quite a battle. You may be saying, "Tony, I've tried to live free of my fleshly desires and operate from my new nature, but the flesh keeps winning."

Engaging the Spirit with Your Mind

The reason so many Christians say that is because they leave out a very important step in the process. Walking by the Spirit in a case like this isn't complete until we come to the Lord and pray, "Lord, I believe what You say about me, and in my mind I want to live for You and obey You.

"Lord, I am going to take a step of faith and turn away from what my flesh is telling me to do. I know this pleases You, but You also know that I don't have the ability to pull off what I have just determined to do in my mind. So I am relying on the power of Your Holy Spirit to enable me to walk in the direction that You want me to go."

When you engage the Spirit in your mind, the fleshly feelings may still be there, but they will lose their power. God will empower you not to carry out the desires of the flesh.

Your mind is like a radio with two stations, the Heavenly Broadcasting Network and the Fleshly Broadcasting Network. Both stations are sending out signals, and they're conflicting.

The fleshly network is working your emotions, sending out the message, "Feels good, looks good, tastes good, must be good. Go ahead and take it."

But the heavenly network is saying, "Is it true? Does it conform to God's will and the character of Christ? If it's not true, better leave it alone. You don't need it."

This doesn't mean the flesh never uses truth. The flesh will distort and twist the truth to its own advantage. And it doesn't mean the Spirit-directed life is devoid of any feeling or emotion.

The issue is which one will become the basis of your thinking. If it's your fleshly feelings, you'd better be very careful, because the flesh's desire is to kill your spiritual progress. Besides, if you lean solely on your feelings, the flesh will almost always win, because feelings are powerful. If you don't believe this, just think of the Christians who have deliberately sinned in the face of the truth, going against everything they know to be true, simply because that's what they wanted to do.

In case setting your mind on Christ sounds a little too "otherworldly" for the nitty-gritty of everyday life, let me remind you that through your new identity in Christ, you *are* otherworldly. You are now seated with Him in heavenly places. You are operating by a higher law, so don't let the gravitational pull of the flesh drag you down.

THE POWER OF WALKING BY THE SPIRIT

There is power in walking by the Spirit—and it's a good thing, because we are in a spiritual war. "The flesh sets its desire against the Spirit, and the Spirit against the flesh; for these are in opposition to one another, so that you may not do the things that you please" (Galatians 5:17).

The War Within

We need to learn to walk by the Spirit because we have two forces at war with each other in the same house—our flesh, our bodies. Some married couples know what this means because even though they live in the same house, they can't get along. They can't stand each other.

That's the battle between the flesh and the Spirit, and it will never be resolved in this life because these two are set in determined, deadly opposition to each other.

Every time your flesh seeks to express itself in a sinful way, the Spirit of God is going to go into action and set Himself against that desire.

That's why we feel guilty when we do wrong or contemplate doing wrong. In fact, one way you know you're saved is that this battle goes on within you. Lost people don't have this same battle because they are dead to the Spirit and at the mercy of the world, the flesh, and the devil.

Christians are capable of committing any sin that a non-Christian can commit—except that we can't do it without a battle erupting in our minds, because the Spirit and the flesh are set in opposition to each other.

We know that the flesh is strong, but, praise God, the Spirit is infinitely stronger. So when you set your mind on the Spirit and determine to live God's way, you have the most incredible power in the universe at your disposal. You have available to you the power that raised Jesus from the grave!

No, that doesn't mean the flesh is going to quit and go home. Your flesh will still get in the way and try to bring you down when you determine you are going to walk by the Spirit.

Sometimes the flesh strikes at the most unlikely times, such as in the church parking lot on your way home from Sunday services. You go out of church rejoicing in the Lord and on fire for Christ—and somebody cuts you off in the parking lot. Or your spouse says something and you go off. And your spiritual vitality evaporates as the flesh rears its ugly head.

To be sure, walking by the Spirit and engaging His power is not a guarantee that the flesh will never win a skirmish here and there. You may even lose a few battles. But you don't have to lose the war, because you can choose to live based on your new identity in Christ.

Until we learn how to live by the power of the Holy Spirit, we'll keep attacking the wrong enemy. If you're struggling with a spiritual conflict and losing to the flesh, then changing cities, jobs, friends—or even mates—won't solve your problem, because the flesh has you.

The Anointing Is on You

One Sunday, during the time I was teaching these concepts at our church in Dallas, we sang a song that asked God to "let the anointing fall on me."

Suddenly, it occurred to me that even though this is a great song, it misses a major truth. You see, when we ask God to let the Spirit's anointing, a synonym for His power and presence, fall on us, this gives the impression that it's out in space somewhere and needs to be prayed down into our lives.

When I heard that song, my mind turned to 1 John 2:27, which is addressed to believers: "As for you, the anointing which you received from Him abides in you." If you know Christ, you don't need the Spirit's anointing to fall on you. It fell on you the moment you trusted Christ and were saved, and it has never left, because the anointing is the Holy Spirit's presence in your life.

I was thinking of a way to illustrate this when I saw the satellite dishes that dot many of the roofs and yards in my neighborhood. A satellite dish is a built-in receiver for an unseen signal, and whenever the signal is sent out the dish picks it up, translates it, and delivers the desired result, a ball game or some other program.

A satellite dish is like the Spirit's anointing. That is, the Spirit's job is to pick up the unseen signal from God and translate that signal into power you can use every day to achieve the desired result of living for Christ.

So don't think the Spirit and His power are "out there" somewhere, beyond your reach in the daily battles you face with the flesh. Jesus said, "'He who believes in Me, as the Scripture said, "From his innermost being will flow rivers of living water."' But this He spoke of the Spirit" (John 7:38–39a). The Spirit resides in our innermost being. We have a built-in filling station that is always pumping fresh life into us.

How do we get the Spirit's power? Not by being "slain in the Spirit" and lying on the floor twitching. The Spirit wants to take some of the people who were knocked down and help them to live right when they get up. The Spirit's power comes through the moment-by-moment experience of being filled with Him.

THE PROCESS OF WALKING BY THE SPIRIT

In a verse that is very familiar to many Christians, the Bible tells us, "Do not get drunk with wine, for that is dissipation, but be filled with the Spirit" (Ephesians 5:18). This brief statement is packed with important principles to help you walk by the Spirit each day.

Who Needs to Be Filled

The fact that this verse is stated in the form of a command ought to be the most encouraging news in the world to us. It means that being filled with the Spirit is not only God's will for us, but it is achievable. The Bible would never issue a command we did not have the ability to obey, even if our obedience will be imperfect in this life.

Allowing the Holy Spirit to fill us is a choice we can make in our will. You can be filled anytime you want to be filled, and for as long as you want to be filled.

The point is, we really don't have any excuses for living in spiritual weakness. If my car is low on gas, I can sit in the driveway and fret about it or I can go to the gas station and fill up.

A second feature of the verse isn't obvious in the English text, but this command is plural. We could translate it, "All of you, be filled with the Spirit." This is not a super spirituality for the elite few. The Spirit-filled Christian life is the normal Christian life.

Here's a third important feature of this verse: The command is passive. You don't fill yourself. God does the work. All you have to do is cooperate with Him.

Fourth, the form of the command teaches us that the Spirit's filling is continuous. This isn't something you do once for all. The command could be translated, "Keep on being filled with the Spirit." This is a day-by-day, even moment-by-moment, reality. The Spirit's filling can run low, so to speak, as we go through life's experiences. But we can at any moment yield ourselves in a new way to the Spirit's filling.

What It Means to Be Filled

The Bible compares being filled with the Spirit to being drunk with wine. The reason is that when a person drinks, he comes under the influence of the alcohol. People often change radically when they're under the influence of alcohol. A quiet person may become loud. A person who can't sing thinks he's Pavarotti. People don't act like they would normally act.

God wants us to come under the influence of the Spirit to such a degree that we come totally under His influence. But how do we get filled with the Spirit?

I only know one way, and that's to saturate ourselves with the Spirit the way drunks saturate their bodies with beer or wine. The way to get drunk is to drink a lot and keep on drinking. Taking a small sip of alcohol every Sunday and Wednesday will not lead to drunkenness.

Do you get the point? We want to "sip" the Spirit and then live a Spirit-filled life. But God is not interested in our taking an occasional sip. He wants us to take in the Spirit the way a drunk takes to the bottle.

How do we do that? Paul told us. "Speaking to one another in psalms and hymns and spiritual songs, singing and making melody with your heart to the Lord; always giving thanks for all things in the name of our Lord Jesus Christ" (Ephesians 5:19–20).

To be filled with the Spirit, make worship a lifestyle. The benediction on Sunday morning is not a signal that worship has now ended. God wants you to carry the worship out to the parking lot and into your home and onto the job Monday morning.

Why do we need to make worship a way of life? Because as we suggested above, the Spirit's filling is not a one-time deal. God commands us to set our minds on the things of Christ (Colossians 3:2) because our minds tend to wander. We need to keep on being filled with the Holy Spirit because our spiritual tanks tend to run dry as we live in a secular, godless age.

THE PRODUCTIVITY OF WALKING BY THE SPIRIT

What kinds of things begin to happen when we learn to walk by the Spirit, filled with His power and praise and worshiping God as a way of life? We start producing spiritual fruit that nourishes us and makes other people want to taste what we have.

For this we turn back to Galatians 5:22–23, another very familiar passage that tells us what a Spirit-filled Christian looks like. If you want to get the full impact, start reading at verse 19 and review "the deeds of the flesh."

Fleshly Deeds Versus the Spirit's Fruit

Notice a few contrasts between these deeds and the fruit of the Spirit. We can do the flesh's deeds on our own, without any help, but we can't grow fruit on our own. Fruit only grows in the right conditions, and even then we can't force it to grow.

The flesh's deeds will leave us with a bitter and empty taste in our mouths. But fruit is sweet and enjoyable, not only to us but to anybody else we share it with.

The deeds of the flesh can also be produced in isolation, without any vital connection to anything. But fruit has to be connected to a tree or a vine to flourish.

One Unusual Fruit Tree

Paul used the singular word *fruit*, even though nine qualities are listed, because the Spirit's work in our lives is like a fruit tree you have never seen before. All other trees produce just one kind of fruit, but not this tree. It produces a rich selection, all from the same root.

A WONDERFUL DISCOVERY

We've seen that the Bible uses a variety of physical things to describe the spiritual life God wants us to enjoy: the act of walking, our minds, fruit, and even the effects of drinking. All of these are pointing to the same reality. When we decide to "live by the Spirit" (Galatians 5:25), He will scrub out all the junk in our lives and make us clean, ready to be receptacles of His fullness.

My wife loves to keep a clean house, to put it mildly. She will clean anything, but she hates to scrub the bathtub. When we got married, Lois only asked me to do two things around the house: take out the trash and clean the bathtub. So I always tried to make sure we rented apartments with showers only!

If you have ever cleaned a bathtub, you know that it's no fun. It's uncomfortable leaning over on your knees, and it takes a lot of hard scrubbing to get that ring out.

But then I went to the store one day and made a wonderful discovery. I found a new product that you simply spray on the ring and rinse off after it has done its cleaning work.

If you are tired of trying to scrub your life clean in the energy of your flesh, I have good news for you. You need to apply the Holy

Spirit to that mess. He will bubble it all away and make you a clean receptacle, ready to be filled and used for the Lord. What are you waiting for?

Chapter Ten

LIVING BY FAITH

If you have a computer at your office or at home with valuable information on it that needs to be protected, chances are you have set up your computer with a password that gives you access to your files while keeping the wrong people out.

We have been learning throughout this book that God has given us something of great value, our identity in Jesus Christ as saints who are risen and seated with Him in heavenly places. That's the most valuable information you could ever receive. There is so much available to us in Christ that we will spend eternity enjoying Him and understanding what He did for us.

If you are a Christian, what God says about you is already true. But we must also realize that *possessing* all we have in Christ and *accessing* those blessings in our daily experience are not the same thing. The possessions are ours; benefiting from them to the full is up to us.

I know some believers are not accessing all they have. I know that because I see too many Christians who have been set free from every shackle and are incredibly spiritually wealthy in Christ but who are dragging around the chains of bondage and settling for a pauper's paradise.

But God has not only given us every spiritual blessing. He has also given us the password that opens the riches of Christ to us. This password is *faith*.

A DESCRIPTION OF FAITH

There are a number of ways we could define faith. In an earlier chapter, I defined faith as simply acting as if God is telling the truth.

The Faith Connection

Faith is the wire over which the current of God's grace travels to bring you the privileges of your identity in Christ. Your provision of those privileges comes by grace, but access to your provision comes through faith. We could say that grace gives you what you have; faith enables you to experience what grace gives you.

Let me make clear right away that we are not talking about saving faith, but the faith that undergirds our daily Christian lives. Every true Christian has the same measure of grace. God does not give some people more grace than others because He likes them better. But believers do not all enjoy or use the blessings of grace to an equal degree, because faith requires a response on our part.

I need to make another disclaimer before we go on. The doctrine of faith is being tossed around pretty loosely these days and getting twisted and confused in the process. According to the so-called health-and-wealth gospel, the "name it and claim it" crowd, our only problem is that we always need more faith. If you don't get your miracle today, it's because you don't have enough faith. I'll have more to say about this later, so suffice it to say here that I'm not talking about faith as a magic wand we wave before God in such an irresistible way that He just can't help but give us whatever we want from Him. That is a distortion of biblical faith.

Real-World Faith

Having said that, however, it is my intention in this chapter to show you the vital part that faith plays in the Christian life. In fact, faith plays a big part not just in our spiritual lives, but in other areas.

All of us, atheists included, go to the doctor by faith. We believe the doctor has the proper training and knows what he or she is doing. Doctors use words we don't understand that they learned in books we have never read, yet on their word alone we take a piece of paper to the pharmacy and believe that the medicine we receive will benefit us. We also trust the pharmacist to fill our prescription correctly.

So don't let anyone tell you that faith is some ethereal, cloudy concept that has no place in the real world. It has every place. As a matter of fact, faith *is* the real world. Let's find out what this biblical password means and what it unlocks for us. The moment you read the title of this chapter, you may have thought of Hebrews 11, the Bible's great faith chapter. Hebrews 11 is "faith concentrate," a passage that's packed with principles and real-life examples of faith.

THE MEANING OF FAITH

What do we mean by faith? The closest the Bible comes to a definition of faith is the opening verse of Hebrews 11. "Now faith is the assurance of things hoped for, the conviction of things not seen."

The King James Version translates the word *assurance* as "substance." Faith is not some hazy concept hanging out there on nothing. It has substance to it. Another word for substance might be "stuff." Faith is related to stuff, to something really concrete.

So when someone says you need to have faith, your question should be, "Faith in what? What is the stuff you're asking me to have faith in?" If someone expects me to believe in something that is not a worthy and reliable object of faith, I'm going to have a serious problem.

I got a firsthand illustration of this one day on the streets of New York City. A street vendor was selling watches, and as I walked by he showed me the watches on his arm and said, "Hey, man, this is real silver and real gold." Now this particular merchant did not look like somebody who would be handling significant amounts of silver and gold, so the longer I looked at those watches, the weaker my faith became. I decided his stuff was not worthy of my trust.

In one sense, faith isn't the significant issue—it's *where* your faith rests that's important. So what is it that we are called to believe? Simply stated, we are called to believe the revelation of God, even when His truth contradicts what we can see and touch and measure.

Admittedly, that's not always easy to do, because we are earthbound creatures. This is the dilemma of faith. We must choose between what God says is true, even when we can't see it, and what we *can* see and that looks more true than what God says.

This was Eve's dilemma in the Garden of Eden (Genesis 3:1–7). She had God's word that the Tree of the Knowledge of Good and Evil held death for her if she touched it. But the tree looked good to Eve—so desirable that she chose to believe the serpent and her eyes instead of God's revelation.

Let me relate this to our identity in Christ. Peter began his second letter by greeting the saints. Then he wrote:

> Grace and peace be multiplied to you in the knowledge of God and of Jesus our Lord; seeing that His divine power has granted to us everything pertaining to life and godliness, through the true knowledge of Him who called us by His own glory and excellence. For by these He has granted to us His precious and magnificent promises, so that by them you may become partakers of the divine nature. (vv. 2–4)

Peter is saying that through His promises, God has supplied us with every possible thing we could ever need. We have these promises as bearers of the "divine nature," which is our new identity in Christ. Peter's prayer is that we as believers will experience to the full these precious promises God has given us. How do you experience a promise someone has made to you? By believing it and acting on it in faith. God wants us to take His promises as certain because they are tied to His infinite Person, and He has the ability to pull off what He promises. The only issue for us is, Do we believe what God has said?

THE IMPORTANCE OF FAITH

You may have memorized Hebrews 11:6 at one time. "Without faith it is impossible to please Him, for he who comes to God must believe that He is and that He is a rewarder of those who seek Him."

This is as strong a statement of the importance of faith as you will find in God's Word.

The Results of Faith

If we want to please God, we had better know how to exercise faith. It's not hard to please God without faith—it's *impossible.* Not only that, but it's impossible to expect anything from Him without faith, for we must believe Him before He becomes our "rewarder."

There's a good example of this earlier in Hebrews. The writer spoke of those in Israel who made God's Word ineffective in their lives by a lack of faith. They heard "the good news," but failed to benefit from it. Why? "Because it [the good news] was not united by faith in those who heard" (4:1–2).

Notice the situation here. The Word of God is alive and powerful (see Hebrews 4:12), so that was not the problem. But the people of Israel didn't mix faith into the formula. Result—nothing. So when we come to God devoid of faith, instead of making God happy we make Him unhappy, and instead of receiving His good gifts those blessings are withheld.

This means if we come to church and hear the Word of God, but leave without faith, we have just wasted two hours, because God is not impressed with activity. If faith is missing from our lives in terms of acting as if God is telling the truth, nothing else we do matters much.

The writer of Hebrews built up to the great faith chapter by making some very important statements about faith in Hebrews 10:

> Therefore, do not throw away your confidence, which has a great reward. For you have need of endurance, so that when you have done the will of God, you may receive what was promised. . . . But My righteous one shall live by faith; and if he shrinks back, My soul has no pleasure in him. (vv. 35–36, 38)

Notice that the same themes of the centrality of faith, pleasing or displeasing God, and gaining a reward are here, just as they are in Hebrews 11:6.

Linking Two Worlds

Why is faith the password for a life that pleases God and wins His blessing? One reason is that faith links the invisible with the visible, the "things not seen" with "what is seen" (Hebrews 11:1, 3), opening our eyes to the invisible God behind the things that are visible.

Verse 3 gives us an example in the creation. "By faith we understand that the worlds were prepared by the word of God, so that what is seen was not made out of things which are visible." We weren't there at the beginning, and neither was the evolutionary scientist who assumes there was no Creator. We take God at His word by faith when He says He spoke the worlds into existence by the word of His power.

Many visible things in creation point back to God as the Creator, but faith is still required to believe that what God says, He is also able to perform (see Romans 4:18–21).

Who's Telling the Truth?

Let's get real bottom line here. Faith, or the lack thereof, is our statement about who's telling the truth and who's lying. When God says something and we don't believe it, we are in essence saying, "God, You're a liar."

Does that sound too strong? God said, "All have sinned" (Romans 3:23). So the apostle John said, "If we say we have not sinned, we make Him a liar" (1 John 1:10).

We would never call God a liar in so many words, but that's what we're saying when we refuse to live by faith. The Bible says it is "impossible" for God to lie, so guess who has the problem if we aren't willing to act on His Word in faith? Paul capped it all when he declared, "Let God be found true, though every man be found a liar" (Romans 3:4).

My point is that faith is critical, because without it we cannot please God and we impugn His character.

THE FOCUS OF FAITH

This brings us to the issue of faith's focus. Even great faith focused on the wrong object will get us nowhere.

Whom Are You Going to Believe?

Here's how this often works in our day-to-day experience. God has said that I am a brand-new creation in Jesus Christ. But I say, "Lord, I don't feel like a new creation. The old urges are strong. Satan and my flesh say I'm the same old person, that I'm just fooling myself."

God says, "Whom are you going to believe?"

Here's another one. God says I can do anything through Christ's strength (Philippians 4:13). God even says I can "overwhelmingly conquer" because Christ loves me (Romans 8:37).

But I get up one morning and say, "Lord, I don't feel like a conqueror today. In fact, I feel more than conquered today. I feel like a loser. Look at what I'm going through right now. My circumstances are telling me I can't possibly do what You say I can do."

God's response is, "Whom are you going to believe?"

Feelings or Faith?

You see, Satan knows that if he can get us focused on our feelings and our five senses instead of focusing on God in faith, we will veer off the highway of faith onto the shoulder of doubt. Then we will meander along day after day, week after week in spiritual defeat, wondering why God isn't coming through for us. God's answer is, "Because you are not treating Me as God. I reward faith."

One of the leading causes of spiritual defeat in our lives is trusting what we feel over what God says. Too many believers rely on their feelings to define their reality. So if they feel worthless or depressed or hopeless, that's the way they operate. It works the other way too. There are times we feel good about things we shouldn't feel good about. Eve began to feel so good about the forbidden tree that she ignored what God said. When you start living by your feelings instead of by faith, all Satan has to do to keep you off balance is to keep your feelings stirred up. And for most of us, that's not all that hard to do.

God will sometimes allow the devil to stir up our feelings to drive us to faith. This happens when people begin to doubt their salvation.

My experience as a pastor has been that few people who struggle with doubt do so because they have become thoroughly and sincerely convinced that God's Word is not true. The problem usually is that they don't *feel* saved because of hard times or spiritual failure or something else.

When those feelings of doubt come, they seldom leave just because the doubter starts to feel better. Doubts are usually settled when the Holy Spirit takes a believer to God's Word and drives home the truth of God's promises in a new way, giving that person a new sense of peace and assurance. Feelings of doubt are not from God, but He can use them to strengthen our faith.

Acting on What God Says

Faith is like a radio that picks up an invisible signal and translates it into programming you can hear and enjoy. You might say the radio acts on what the transmitter says.

Faith operates on what God says and then trusts God to change the feelings. You may not feel victorious, but by an act of faith you can engage your will to believe what God has said.

You may say, "Tony, that sounds like positive thinking, trying to convince yourself something is true."

No, not at all. We're talking here about a faith that has a particular focus, in this case, the eternally truthful God and His Word. If God says something is true, then you have to decide whether you are going to believe it. Most Christians spend their lives adjusting their faith to match their feelings, rather than adjusting their feelings to match what God has said.

When you put your money in a bank, you need to know if the bank is able to keep your money secure and give you adequate interest on your deposits. If not, rather than lying awake at night worrying about your money, you need to find another bank. If the object of your trust can't handle what you have deposited in it, you need a more reliable object of trust.

You Don't Need More Faith

This leads to one of the great misconceptions people have about the Christian life. The misconception is that if your Christian life is not all it should be, or if you're not seeing answers to your prayers, the problem is that you need more faith. This has been the standard line of argument for years among many of the proponents of prosperity theology. If you want your miracle today, you have to show God how badly you want it—usually by sending the teacher a financial gift to get things rolling.

God gave us all the faith we needed when He saved us.

Let me take that load off you right now. You don't need more faith. You just need to exercise the faith God has already given you.

How do I know this? Because the one time the disciples asked Jesus to give them more faith, He responded, "If you had faith like a mustard seed, you would say to this mulberry tree, 'Be uprooted and be planted in the sea'; and it would obey you" (Luke 17:6; note also v. 5). In another place, He said that mustard-seed faith will move mountains (Matthew 17:20).

Don't miss what Jesus said. He denied the disciples' request for more faith, saying in effect, "The faith you have is big enough to remove any obstacle."

This idea that you don't need more faith may seem a little foreign to you. Didn't Jesus tell the disciples more than once that their faith was too small?

Yes, He did. In fact, He prefaced His statement about mustard-seed faith in Matthew 17:20 by telling the disciples they could not help a demon-possessed boy "because of the littleness of [their] faith."

But Jesus wasn't saying they needed more faith in the sense that the "name it, claim it" emphasis teaches. This teaching implies that the faith we received at salvation is somehow partial or inadequate and needs more faith added to it.

But Jesus said the exact opposite. The amount of faith isn't the issue. God gave us all the faith we needed when He saved us, because the Bible says He has given us *everything* we need for life and godliness.

The issue is what we do with our faith. Instead of saying we need more faith, it would be more biblical to say we need to strengthen the faith we already have.

STRENGTHENING YOUR FAITH

How can you strengthen your faith? I want to suggest that the best way is by increasing or strengthening your knowledge of Jesus Christ, the focus and object of the Christian's faith.

Getting to Know God

That means immersing yourself in God's Word, because "Faith comes from hearing, and hearing by the word of Christ" (Romans 10:17). By this I don't mean just spending more time reading and studying the Bible, although that would be a great place to start. I'm talking about getting to know and love the God of the Word so intimately that you come to trust Him implicitly.

Learning from the example of the saints is also a great way to strengthen your faith. That's why Hebrews 11 was written.

The author of Hebrews was not just demonstrating how much he knew about the Old Testament. He was saying to the wavering Hebrews, "Look at the way the saints of old remained true to the Lord by faith. You can do it too, so hang in there and don't throw away your confidence in God's promises."

The story is told of a man out on the frontier whose wife fell deathly ill. He set out on foot to reach a nearby settlement where there was medicine that would save his wife's life. But it was wintertime, and to reach the settlement he had to cross a frozen lake.

The man stopped at the edge of the lake, unsure that the ice would support his weight. But since his wife's life was at stake, he had no choice but to try. He got down on his hands and knees and began inching his way across the ice, terrified that it would break at any moment and he would sink to his death. All of a sudden, he heard a loud rumbling on the ice. At first he thought it was the ice cracking, and he became more scared than ever.

But as the sound got closer, the man looked behind him and, to his astonishment, saw a wagon with a team of horses coming across the ice. As the wagon passed him and went on over the lake, this formerly fearful husband stood up and began to run with abandon across the ice. He knew if the ice could hold a team of horses, it could certainly hold him.

Putting Your Confidence in God

If you want to have more confidence in God, then hang around people who have been ahead of you on the ice and have proved Him faithful. Get to know God as He reveals Himself in His Word, and your faith will grow stronger. Peter said that we know what God has given us through "the knowledge of God and of Jesus our Lord," and again "through the true knowledge of Him who called us" (2 Peter 1:2–3).

The man in the previous illustration changed his feelings about the ice because his knowledge of the ice changed. A good Old Testament illustration of this is Israel on the evening of the Passover in Egypt (Exodus 12:1–36).

Trust God and Go to Bed

God had told the Israelites to put the blood of the Passover lamb on the doorposts of their homes so the death angel would pass over them and not strike the firstborn child dead.

Imagine a firstborn son in one of those Jewish homes. His father has told him what God said about the death angel coming that night and how to protect their home by the act of faith of killing a lamb and sprinkling their doorposts.

This son goes to his father and says, "Father, I'm afraid."

His father answers, "Don't be afraid, Son. I put the blood on our doorposts. God will protect us."

"But I'm still afraid, Father. I'm the one who will die tonight if something goes wrong."

So the father reviews God's promise to spare the firstborn in the homes covered by the blood and takes his son outside and shows him the blood dripping down the doorposts. Then he says, "Son, you can either go to sleep tonight, or you can stay awake and worry. But I'm going to bed because I obeyed God, and I believe what He said."

Satan wants to keep you up at night worrying about whether you can trust God to keep His Word. You can either sit up all night wringing your hands and discussing the various aspects of faith, or you can trust God and go to bed.

Faith is measured by what we do, not by what we discuss. All of the heroes in Hebrews 11 are known for what they did, not what they talked about.

Put It in Jesus' Name

Someone may ask, "How do I know when I'm supposed to act in faith regardless of how bad things look?"

Well, one way is to pray about it, and then attach Jesus' name to your prayer and see if it sounds right. For instance, does this sound right? "Lord, I cannot handle this problem. I am totally defeated. There is no way I can make it. I pray all these things in Jesus' name. Amen."

Something doesn't sound right about that, does it? Now try this: "Lord, You said I am an overwhelming conqueror in Jesus' name. I can do all things in Jesus' name. I am victorious in Jesus' name. So I am going to believe You and engage my will to trust You in this circumstance. In Jesus' name. Amen."

Keep Your Eyes on Jesus

In Hebrews 12, the writer transitions from the heroes of faith in the past to the present day. Since we have the testimony of these who have gone before, we need to run the race of the Christian life in a particular way, as verse 2 explains: "[Fix] our eyes on Jesus, the author and perfecter of faith, who for the joy set before Him endured the cross, despising the shame, and has sat down at the right hand of the throne of God."

Don't fix your eyes on how you feel inside or what is happening around you, but fix them on Jesus. Keep your eyes of faith set on God and His promises, and remember that the issue is whom you are going to believe. Faith is no mystical concept. It is simply taking God at His Word and acting in light of that.

When you do this, you will begin to see the invisible world of the Spirit controlling your visible world, and not the other way around (2 Corinthians 4:18; Hebrews 1:3).

Chapter Eleven

REPROGRAMMING YOUR MIND

The Communist government of China has special labor camps for political and religious prisoners whose thinking and ideas are considered a threat to the Marxist cause. A number of Chinese pastors and other Christian leaders have been sentenced to these camps, sometimes for years at a time.

The Chinese have an interesting term for this process. They say the prisoner is being sent to the camp for "reeducation through labor," a pitiful euphemism for an attempt to break prisoners down physically and reprogram their minds through propaganda. The idea is to do whatever it takes to try to remake the prisoner in the Communists' image.

The Chinese government's "reeducation" camps operate on a basic principle that is taught in God's Word, except that the Communists are using it for their twisted, evil purposes. The principle is this: If you want people to think in new ways and in different categories, you have to erase the old ways of thinking from their minds. Their minds must be reprogrammed.

One of the basic theses of this book is that because we are new people in Jesus Christ, with a completely new identity, you and I need to think and live in light of who God says we are. But in case you haven't discovered it yet, living up to your new identity in Christ requires the reprogramming of your mind.

The Bible says we need to be "transformed by the renewing of [o]ur mind" before we will be able to tap into God's good and perfect and pleasing will for us (Romans 12:2). So let's talk about another core issue related to our freedom and our victory in Christ, the reprogramming of our minds.

THE BATTLE FOR THE MIND

The Chinese Communists are deadly serious about their propaganda program because they know that the survival of Marxism depends on capturing people's minds. Even one pastor with a renewed mind, or a political leader who is committed to democracy, is a potential threat to their system.

Since our minds are so crucial to our functioning as Christians, the mind is the devil's number one battlefield. He's not about to let us become new people with renewed minds without putting up a fight.

Locked in Deadly Combat

We keep coming back to Romans 8 for foundational truths about this issue of the Christian mind. Let me remind you briefly that verses 5–6 give us the parameters of the battle for our minds. There are two basic mind-sets, the mind set on the flesh and the mind set on the Spirit.

Paul said the fleshly mind leads to death, whereas the Spirit-directed mind leads to "life and peace." Galatians 5:17 says that these two minds are completely irreconcilable. So the battle is intense, "because the mind set on the flesh is hostile toward God; for it does not subject itself to the law of God, for it is not even able to do so" (Romans 8:7).

Christians who live with a fleshly mind-set live in the realm of death. It kills their joy, their victory, their peace. The life of God will not pulsate through them even though it resides in them. A fleshly mind also kills the freedom that is the birthright of all believers. But Christians whose mind is set on the Spirit will enjoy to the full the abundant, victorious, liberated life that Jesus Christ promised.

The difference between a perpetually defeated believer and a perpetually victorious believer is where they have set their minds. The battle for your mind is a battle between the flesh and the Spirit.

We know that what appears on the screen of a computer is what has been programmed into the computer's memory. A lot of Christians don't like what they see coming up on the screen of their lives, but instead of reprogramming their minds they keep adjusting the screen or rebooting the program.

You can try to adjust or "reboot" the flesh all you want, but nothing will change. It needs to be emphasized again and again that the flesh, our unredeemed humanity, is beyond reclamation and needs to be put to death. It is hostile toward God—and hostility is simply another word for warfare.

No Truce with the Flesh

Imagine an army in the middle of a fierce war sending a message to the enemy that says, "You really need to quit being so hostile. Why don't you stop trying to take over our territory and conquer us, and focus on how you can improve your attitude and start being a little nicer and more cooperative?"

No general in his right mind would expect a message like that to change the mind of his sworn enemy. But that's the message we are sending to our flesh when we focus on trying harder, making resolutions and promises to quit doing this and stop being addicted to that and start doing better.

We're playing into the Enemy's hands when we do that, and the devil is laughing up his sleeve at us because he has us right where he wants us.

Trying to reprogram your flesh to get rid of your sin is like a person on a diet going to an ice cream shop to learn better what he or she needs to avoid. A dieter doing that needs some serious reprogramming of the mind. If you need to avoid ice cream, get out of the ice cream shop. Change your thinking.

The brain is the control center of the body. Your hand doesn't move because it suddenly decides to move. It moves when it receives a signal from your brain. In fact, if your hand or foot or any other body part starts functioning independently of the brain, something is terribly wrong.

What the brain is to the body, the mind is to the soul. It's the control center, so that's where the battle is being waged. If Satan wins my mind, he can control my actions.

This is why the Chinese Communists don't simply say to a pastor, "Stop loving and serving God and holding church services." They arrest the pastor and attempt to reprogram his mind so he no longer wants to love and serve God. If that reprogramming were to work, the Communists could let the pastor go, confident that his actions would change to match his new mind-set.

So, make no mistake—there is a spiritual battle raging for our minds. The tragedy is that the world is often more aware of the battle and more committed to winning it than Christians are.

Since we're engaged in an all-out battle, we had better be finding out who and what we're fighting, how the battlefield is laid out, and what tactics and maneuvers are needed to ensure victory.

The Nature of the Battle

All of these important details are provided for us in one brief but crucial passage of God's Word: 2 Corinthians 10:3–5. We're going to spend some serious time examining these verses. Paul began his discussion of this subject by describing the nature of the battle. Since this fight is not "according to the flesh" (v. 3), fleshly weapons are useless. We know why, because nothing in our flesh is going to help us live victorious lives and draw closer to the Lord.

This battle is located in the mind because it involves "speculations," "knowledge," and "every thought" (v. 5). And if the weapons we are to use are not of the flesh, they must be the weapons of the Holy Spirit. Paul said so in so many words when he wrote, "The weapons of our warfare are not of the flesh, but divinely powerful for the destruction of fortresses" (v. 4).

This word *fortresses* is key to understanding and winning the battle for your mind. You will never be successful in allowing the Holy Spirit to reprogram your mind until the Enemy's fortresses in your mind are torn down.

Satan's Strongholds

What are these fortresses Paul was talking about? The King James Version calls them "strong holds." You've probably seen a fortress in a movie about medieval times. Picture a huge structure made of stone with high walls and towers surrounded by a moat.

Hopelessness is a key element of a stronghold.

Medieval fortresses were built to be impregnable. Just looking up at those massive walls would be intimidating to an enemy soldier standing outside, let alone thinking of trying to scale the walls with ladders and bring the fortress down.

Now transfer that image to the realm of the mind, and you'll have the idea. By the way, I'm going to use the term "stronghold" from here on because I think it conveys the idea Paul had in mind a little better.

God says these strongholds have to be destroyed, so that means He didn't build them. A stronghold is a negative, destructive pattern of thinking that Satan has built in our minds, either through repetition or traumatic experiences or other circumstances. As the old adage says, when you sow a thought, you reap an act; sow an act and you reap a habit; sow a habit, and you reap a character; sow a character, and you reap a destiny.

Once the stronghold is built, it gives the Enemy a place from which to launch further attacks against your mind and a fortification from which to repel your attempts to dislodge him. If you're getting the idea that we aren't going to get very far in the battle for our minds until we deal with satanic strongholds, you're right on target. One reason strongholds are so powerful is that they are so entrenched. I said earlier that these are *patterns* of thinking, not just fleeting thoughts.

Let me give you some examples. For a person who is addicted to drugs or alcohol, the satanic stronghold is not the physical addiction or the act of using the substance. Those are just the products of the stronghold. The stronghold itself is having a wrong mind-set toward drugs or alcohol.

By that I mean Satan builds a stronghold when he convinces a person that his situation is hopeless, that he is a drug addict or an alcoholic by nature and will never be anything else. Once a person starts believing that, it's pretty much all over, because we will always act in accord with who we believe we are.

Hopelessness is a key element of a stronghold. As long as you believe there is hope for you to overcome a wrong way of thinking, you'll keep fighting. But once you believe the battle is hopeless, you'll want to surrender.

Satan wants to force his thinking upon us until we actually come to believe that his lies are true. You can tell when people are being ruled by a satanic stronghold. They say things like, "I can't help myself," "It's not my fault," "I was born this way," or "I'm just a victim."

When we view something as unchangeable that God says is changeable, the Enemy has built a stronghold in our minds.

It doesn't have to be anything as dramatic as drug addiction or alcoholism. Many of us have strongholds of anger or jealousy or lust. "I know I get mad and blow my stack, but that's just the way I am." "I can't help lusting. After all, God gave me these sexual desires."

People who have satanic strongholds come to believe the way they are is the only way they can be. That's why they have such a sense of hopelessness, and that's why they are in bondage.

The disorder of anorexia comes to mind as an example of a stronghold. An anorexic person becomes convinced she is too heavy when she is actually dangerously thin. Putting food in front of her, or putting her in front of a mirror and telling her to take a good look at herself, doesn't help. The anorexic may starve herself to death because of what she believes to be true.

When we allow strongholds to be built in our minds, guess who's manning the walls and the guard towers? The Enemy himself. A stronghold gives him a strong base of operation from which to launch continued attacks against us.

Strongholds are a major issue in the battle for our minds. Strongholds not only take over individuals, they can take over families and churches. A church with a perpetual atmosphere of conflict between leaders and hostility and jealousy in the body is being worked over by Satan for his purposes.

Materials for a Stronghold

Satan gets the material to build his strongholds by the wrong thoughts he plants and cultivates in our minds. The Enemy's strategy is suggested in the first half of 2 Corinthians 10:5: "We are destroying speculations and every lofty thing raised up against the knowledge of God."

You can see the conflict here as Satan raises up his lies in the face of what God says about us and what we know to be true from His Word. What is the "lofty thing" Satan raises up against the knowledge of God? The term means a "partition," or a wall. Germany was divided by a partition called the Berlin Wall for almost forty years. A partition is designed to keep two entities divided and separated.

Satan begins creating a stronghold by erecting a partition in your mind. He wants to keep out the knowledge of God or to keep it so compartmentalized that the Word never reaches to every corner of your life and runs the show.

Satan is deathly afraid of the truth. He knows that once the knowledge of your new identity in Christ becomes the defining principle of your life, he's finished.

You see, the only power Satan has over us is his lies. He can't force us to do or to believe anything. He works by deception, using smoke and mirrors.

Satan doesn't even have to get us to deny the truth. He knows most Christians are not going to come out and say the Bible is not God's Word and Jesus is not God's Son. All Satan has to do is distract us from the truth so that it never gets down deep inside us.

It's like those televisions that have a picture within a picture so you can watch one channel and check out another one at the same time in a window in the corner.

Giving Satan Ground for a Stronghold

The Bible has a word for that in the spiritual realm. It's called being "double-minded" (James 1:8). The problem is that if you try to watch two channels at once, you won't get the full picture of what's happening on either channel. Your attention is divided because you're looking in two directions at once.

If the Enemy can divide your mind by putting up a partition, he has the first wall of his stronghold in place.

The process isn't hard to understand. When a Christian starts saying of a harmful practice, "One time won't hurt me," or "I can handle this," the devil has a piece of ground in the mind on which he can erect a partition. From there it can deteriorate to this: "I'm hooked on this stuff. I'm an addict, and I always will be. There's no hope for me. I might as well give up trying to change."

It doesn't take long for Satan to mess with our minds.

How quickly can Satan start dividing our thinking? In Peter's case, it only took a few minutes. Jesus was with His disciples one day when He asked, "Who do people say that the Son of Man is?" (Matthew 16:13). They gave various answers, then Jesus asked the key question: "But who do you say that I am?" (v. 15).

Peter spoke up. "You are the Christ, the Son of the living God" (v. 16). Jesus affirmed Peter and told him that he had received that truth as a direct revelation from God the Father.

But then Jesus told the disciples that He must go to Jerusalem and be crucified, and an alarm went off in Peter's mind. This didn't make sense to him, so he pulled Jesus aside and rebuked Him. "God forbid it, Lord! This shall never happen to You" (v. 22).

Being the Son of God and being crucified didn't compute to Peter. He began thinking that Jesus was obviously mistaken. Besides, if Jesus got into trouble with the authorities in Jerusalem, His disciples would be in trouble too. So Peter tried to talk Jesus out of going to the cross—and in that instant, Peter bought into Satan's thinking.

That's why Jesus stunned Peter back to reality. "Get behind Me, Satan! You are a stumbling block to Me; for you are not setting your mind on God's interests, but man's" (v. 23).

Jesus hit the issue on the head. Peter was setting his mind on the flesh (remember Romans 8:6), and he was on very dangerous ground. Satan had partitioned Peter's mind so completely that he was thinking in two totally opposite directions at the same time.

It doesn't take long for Satan to mess with our minds. Peter lost it between the time he heard the sermon and the time he reached the parking lot, to put it in church terms. That's how fast it can happen for us.

We can promise God in church that we're not going to lose our temper with the kids or the spouse, and on the way home from church someone says something to set us off. Satan wants to block the flow of truth by dividing our minds so he can get us to believe his lies and allow him to build his strongholds.

REPROGRAMMING YOUR MIND

What needs to be done with Satan's strongholds? You can't go around them, and you can't ignore them, because the Enemy will use them to launch more attacks and build more strongholds.

The only solution is to tear those lofty strongholds down by "taking every thought captive to the obedience to Christ" (2 Corinthians 10:5). This is how to reprogram your mind.

Sorting Out Our Thoughts

Why must we take every thought captive to Christ? Because not every thought that comes into our minds is of God. Strongholds in the mind are built out of the Enemy's thoughts. We are either thinking with the mind of Christ or with a mind set on the world, the flesh, and the devil.

There is no such thing as neutral thoughts. That's why Eastern meditation and thought processes are so dangerous. They teach you to empty your mind and open it up to new ways of thinking. But that is giving the devil a foothold to bring in his thoughts.

We have to capture our thoughts, because if we don't recognize and capture the Enemy's thoughts, he will gain an advantage.

When a thought that's against the knowledge of God comes into your mind, you have two choices. You can capture and destroy it because you know it's not yours, or you can adopt it and act on it until you believe it's really your idea after all. Let's see what it takes to reprogram our minds.

Getting the Facts Straight

Colossians 3 is another passage that is crucial to the process of bringing our thoughts under the authority of Christ and reprogramming our minds. Paul wrote, "If you have been raised up with Christ, keep seeking the things above, where Christ is, seated at the right hand of God" (v. 1). The solution to the problem of wrong thinking is not down here on earth.

That shouldn't surprise us, because as new creations in Christ we are in fact already raised with Him and seated with Him in heavenly places. So we keep coming back to the beginning point, our identity and spiritual position with Christ.

How do you "keep seeking the things above"? Verse 2 of Colossians 3 says, "Set your mind on the things above, not on the things that are on earth." This is starting to sound very familiar, isn't it? The way to destroy Satan's strongholds and capture every thought for Christ is to visualize your spiritual reality.

I know the word *visualize* scares some people because the New Agers do this. But God is not asking you to visualize something that isn't true. He's asking you to set your mind on something that is absolutely true, the truth of your exalted position in Christ.

This goes back to what we talked about earlier—the struggle we often face between what God says is true about us and what we may feel or believe at the moment. This is the point of conflict at which we determine whether we are going to succumb to the lies of Satan or recognize those lies for what they are and destroy them with the truth.

We've given many examples of how this works. The lie is that you're an angry person who can't help exploding whenever someone crosses you. The truth is that as a new person in Christ, you don't have to be in bondage to your anger.

Jesus made a very revealing statement one day. "You will know the truth, and the truth will make you free" (John 8:32). Your power over the devil doesn't come from "power encounters" in which you order the devil to do this or that in Jesus' name. Your power over the devil comes in "truth encounters," because the devil is a liar by nature and can't handle the truth.

Notice carefully what Jesus said. He did not say, "You will *hear* the truth," but "You will *know* the truth." It's the truth you know that frees you.

In other words, if you're a Christian, the fact of your new identity in Christ is true whether you have grasped it or not. True reality for you is located in the heavenly places, not on earth. Once you change the location of your thinking from earth to heaven, you'll start seeing things clearly.

I live in a neighborhood in Dallas that is down in a gully covered with tall trees. Some years ago, we were having trouble with the reception on our television. We couldn't get a clear picture no matter how much we adjusted the set. So we called in a repairman, and he went up on the roof. He messed with the antenna, but nothing changed. The picture was still fuzzy.

After a while he came down and said, "I think I got it." And sure enough, the picture was fine. I asked him what the problem was. He said, "Your problem is your location. These high trees were blocking your reception. I put an extension on your antenna to raise it above the interference so you can receive the signal."

If Satan is blurring your thinking, your problem is not your spouse or your children or your boss. There's no use trying to adjust those things until you raise your spiritual antenna above the interference and tune in to heaven. The fact is that you have a new identity and a new position in Christ.

Igniting the Facts by Faith

When you get the facts straight, you are ready to act on them, to ignite them by faith. Colossians 3:5 tells us, "Consider the members of your earthly body as dead." Dead to what? To sin and impurity, represented by the evils Paul mentioned in this verse.

We've run into this idea before too. To "consider" a fact means to count it to be so. Once you align your thinking with the fact that the old way of thinking you inherited from Adam is not the real you, you are ready to put the facts to work. Your feelings will start falling in line with the truth, instead of determining what is true for you.

Suppose you were being audited by the IRS, and the auditor said, "Well, everything looks to be in good order on your tax returns. Everything adds up, but I'm going to charge you for back taxes with penalty and interest anyway, because I just have this feeling that you didn't pay enough taxes."

At that point you would be saying, "How you feel is irrelevant to this audit. The fact is that you said my tax returns are accurate and I don't owe anything."

Imagine hearing this line from an IRS auditor and saying, "I see. How long have you been feeling this way? Were you raised to feel this way about taxes? Did something happen in your childhood that caused you to live by your feelings toward taxes rather than by the facts?"

That conversation would not take place. Unless you enjoy paying taxes you don't owe, you would demand that the auditor bring his feelings in line with the facts.

The fact is, you are a new person in Christ with a totally new identity. The fact is that you are seated with Christ in heavenly places. The fact is that you are free at last!

Please don't misunderstand. I'm not discounting the value of getting help to deal with things from our past that are troubling us. But there's a difference between learning from the past and living in it.

Paul said that since we have laid aside our old self and put on our new self, we are people with renewed minds (Ephesians 4:20–24). Therefore, we have the ability to lay aside things like anger and dishonesty and unwholesome speech and bitterness (vv. 25–31). We don't have to be controlled by any of these. The process of putting off the old and putting on the new is what I am calling igniting the facts by faith.

Ask the Holy Spirit to reprogram your mind with the facts.

One day my faith was ignited by the facts in a way I will never forget. I was in the sixth grade at Alexander Hamilton Elementary School in Baltimore. We had a bully at our school, a huge guy who was basically eighteen in the sixth grade. You know the type.

Well, this bully decided he didn't like me, and one day he threatened to get me after school. I was terrified. So when the final bell rang, I took off out of the school, but he spotted me and took off after me.

I knew a fact he didn't know, which was that I lived just three blocks from the school. That fact definitely ignited me to have the faith that I could outrun the bully and make it home before he pounded me into the pavement.

I've never been all that fast, but on that day I would have qualified for the Olympics! The bully was closing in on me, but I turned into my front yard and shot into the house before he could catch me. I ran all the way upstairs to my room and collapsed.

I was still feeling fearful. My heart was pounding from fear and my three-block Olympic sprint. But soon my heart slowed down because of a new fact. I was in my house. The bully couldn't get me there. My faith kicked in, so to speak, and I started feeling safe.

Then another fact dawned on me. Not only was I safe at home in my room, but my daddy was home too. That was great, because even if the bully came to my door, he would have to deal with my daddy. So now my faith was really getting ignited.

Before long I was so full of faith I started walking all over the house as if I was really in charge. I could walk around with inner security and confidence because the facts of my situation had changed my feelings and affected my feet.

Is Satan chasing you? Is your heart pounding and your mind gripped with fear because the bully has you convinced there's no way you can escape from him?

If you belong to Christ, that simply is not true. Ask the Holy Spirit to reprogram your mind with the facts, and then start acting like those facts are true. Not only will your fear leave, but God will build strongholds of truth in your mind and man the guard towers Himself.

That's exactly what He promised in His Word. "The peace of God, which surpasses all comprehension, will guard your hearts and your minds in Christ Jesus" (Philippians 4:7). That word *guard* means to do sentry duty, to stand guard. In Colossians 3:15, Paul said God's peace will "rule" in our hearts.

Don't ever buy Satan's lie that your situation is hopeless or unchangeable. The fact is, "[You] can do all things through Him who strengthens [you]" (Philippians 4:13).

Chapter Twelve

THE POWER OF INTIMACY

Many longtime married couples will attest to the fact that intimacy is one of the first qualities in a marriage to deteriorate if it is not cultivated. That's ironic because for most young couples in a serious dating or courtship relationship, it's this very quality of intimacy that makes everything so special and so exciting.

Before marriage, there is the romantic and emotional intimacy of being together—sharing thoughts and dreams and laughter and just delighting in each other's presence. The intimacy continues even when the two are apart as they talk on the phone or write each other and get lost in their thoughts of the other person. And even in a sexually pure premarital relationship, there is the intimacy of an arm around the shoulder and a kiss.

If you dated in the days before seat belts, you remember sitting as close as possible to your beloved. In fact, in those days you could tell when a couple wasn't getting along, because the girl would be sitting as close to the passenger door as she could get.

Another thing that is usually true of those early, exhilarating days of first love is that relationship is dominant over performance. By that I mean the girl might say, "Honey, I need to tell you I'm not exactly the best cook in the world."

He didn't hear a word she said. He's so entranced by her eyes and the cute way she talks that her cooking ability is totally irrelevant to him.

It works the other way too. The guy may have an entry-level job, or be in school, and be barely able to afford gas, a burger, and a movie. But she treasures the ticket stub from their first date like it was a diamond engagement ring.

And then when a couple comes together in the sacred bond of marriage, their joy is multiplied as they discover the joy and intimacy of a committed, one-flesh physical relationship.

Now the honeymoon stage of marriage comes to an end, and that's OK, because it isn't meant to last. But while the newness of a relationship may wear off, the intimacy doesn't have to fade. In fact, God's purpose for marriage is that a couple's intimacy—true oneness of heart and spirit and body—should deepen and become richer with the passing of time.

Intimacy is one of the greatest delights and blessings that two people in a close relationship can have. The capacity to draw close to another person and share your lives in such a way that you know each through and through is part of the image of God that we bear as human beings.

Now let me ask you a question. If God designed us with a deep need and deep desire for intimacy in our human relationships, and if intimacy reflects God's image within us, what do you suppose God is seeking in His relationship with us? God desires the intimacy of a close relationship with us more than He desires our performance for Him.

The rest of God's creation performs for Him, but the intimacy of relationship with Him is reserved for the people who know Christ as their Savior and have a new identity in Him.

We often hear the question asked, "If you knew that God Himself was waiting to talk and fellowship with you, would you be eager to meet with Him?" I hope the answer to that question is yes, because God *does* desire, even yearns for, an intimate spiritual relationship with His children.

I want to look at three passages of Scripture that teach this truth, a vital part of our freedom in Christ.

You see, one of the beautiful things about true intimacy is that it sets people free. Two people who know each other intimately are free to be themselves around each other. They feel no pressure to prove anything by trying to meet a performance standard or by trying to be someone they aren't.

So if the desire of your heart is to be free at last in your Christian life, I recommend that you begin developing an intimate, rich, freeing, spiritually satisfying love relationship with your Savior and Lord.

THE PASSION OF INTIMACY

Intimacy definitely involves passion, of which physical passion is just one component. That's usually the aspect we think of first, but it's not as important as spiritual intimacy.

As new creations in Christ Jesus, our relationship with Him should be marked by a never-ending passion to know Him better and draw closer to Him. This is my definition of passion: an all-consuming drive to get closer to, and to know more fully, the person with whom we wish to be intimate.

Paul had that kind of passion to know Christ intimately. We know because the apostle told us so in his classic statement of relationship versus performance in Philippians 3:4–14.

We've touched on this famous passage a couple of times. But I want to dig a little deeper into it and see how Paul redirected the passion of his life from his Jewish laws, rules, and performance to his commitment to know Christ.

The Right Kind of Passion

The context here is important, because the chapter begins with a warning about "dogs" and "the false circumcision" (Philippians 3:2). These were the Judaizers who came around trying to get the Philippians passionate about rule-keeping rather than about their relationship with Christ. But Paul was going to say that the power of the Christian life is in knowing Christ (see v. 10).

Philippians 3:3 is a concise description of the Christian life. "We are the true circumcision, who worship in the Spirit of God and glory in Christ Jesus and put no confidence in the flesh."

What a classic statement of the value of the Person of Christ over religious performance. I hope that by now you are seeing a biblical pattern when it comes to the flesh. The only answer for the flesh is to nail it to the cross of Christ. Anyone who is confident of being able to live for Christ in the energy of the flesh is doomed to spiritual defeat.

An Amazing Spiritual Journey

In verse 4 of Philippians 3, Paul began a digression that took him through verse 6, a review of his credentials as a "Jew of Jews," one of the brightest young stars in the contemporary Jewish world.

The argument was straightforward and irrefutable. If fleshly standards of performance, even religious passion, could win God's favor, Paul would have been at the head of the line to get into heaven. The man had a résumé no one could match:

> [I was] circumcised the eighth day, of the nation of Israel, of the tribe of Benjamin, a Hebrew of Hebrews; as to the Law, a Pharisee; as to zeal, a persecutor of the church; as to the righteousness which is in the Law, found blameless. (Philippians 3:5–6)

Nothing was missing in Paul's religious upbringing. He came from the right family, and he had all the little medals for perfect synagogue attendance. He had been made a part of the covenant nation of Israel through the rite of circumcision.

Paul also came from the right side of the tracks. The men of Benjamin's tribe were warriors, the ones who stayed faithful when the rest of the nation turned left on God. Paul had all of the ingredients to be a Jew among Jews, at the top of the heap.

This brilliant Jewish man put his advantages to work. He became a Pharisee, the pinnacle of the religious hierarchy. He studied the Law. He may have memorized the Pentateuch, the five books of Moses. He could say he scrupulously kept the Law, and when a sacrifice needed to be offered, he was there with it.

And Paul didn't do all of this with a yawn, either. He was so on fire for his Pharisaic Judaism that he said, "Let me round up these Christians. I'll hunt all of them down. If you want someone to stamp out this new cult, I'm your man."

There was only one thing Paul was missing. He didn't know Christ, so all of his credentials were useless before God. This idea is hard for people today to accept because our entire culture is driven by performance. How well you do determines your raises and promotions at work, your acceptance in many social circles, and maybe even your acceptance at home.

But spiritual reality hit Paul between the eyes that day when he hit the dirt on his way to Damascus as Jesus arrested him and saved him (Acts 9:1–9). Now Paul could say, "But whatever things were gain to me, those things I have counted as loss for the sake of Christ" (Philippians 3:7).

When Paul met Jesus on the Damascus road, he had to leave all of his religious pride and performance lying there in the dust. He had to face the same realization all sinners must face, that the only way to heaven is a Person, not a performance sheet.

Toss out the Rubbish

Have you come to the realization that your only hope of salvation is to bow before Jesus Christ totally empty-handed and throw yourself on the grace of God?

I pray that you have, because if you are counting on anything else to get you to heaven, I have bad news for you. God's only performance standard is absolute perfection, and you don't qualify. Neither do I. You are saved by trusting Christ to be your Sin-Bearer and to forgive you of your sins.

You may say, "Tony, I already know the Lord. What does all of this have to do with me now?" Everything. Keep reading in Philippians 3. "More than that, I count all things to be loss in view of the surpassing value of knowing Christ Jesus my Lord" (v. 8).

There's a difference between these verses. In verse 7, Paul said "I have counted" everything as loss for Christ, past perfect tense. In verse 8, "I count" everything as loss for Christ, present tense. The first reference is to what has happened since he got saved years earlier, whereas the second was his present experience.

What I want you to see is the extent of Paul's passion to know Christ intimately—because, remember, this is all heading toward a climactic statement in verse 10. Paul said in effect, "I met a Person who will take me to heaven, and I'm still getting to know this Person who makes me powerful and victorious on earth."

To Paul, "the surpassing value of knowing Christ Jesus my Lord" was so life-transforming that all the other stuff became like a heap of smelly manure. That's the literal meaning of "rubbish," which is a more sanitized translation. Why did Paul use this term for his fleshly accomplishments, instead of saying they were OK in themselves but not adequate?

Because he wanted to make sure that neither he, nor the Philippian believers, nor we would ever entertain the thought of relying on ourselves and what we can do to please God. Paul knew that if people hold onto those things, they will lose something of infinitely greater value.

You see, no one wants to brag about manure. You don't attach surpassing value to a heap of dung. That's the point Paul was making. If it's manure, you'll be repulsed by it.

To change the analogy, he had drunk deeply at the poisoned stream of man-made righteousness, and apart from God's grace it would have killed him. So he put up a warning sign so no one else would come behind him and drink from the same stream. When the Bible tells us not to put any confidence in the flesh, you can put a period after the sentence. End of discussion.

What We Need to Know About Christ

The power to live for Christ comes from knowing the Person of Christ and from receiving the righteousness that comes only through faith in Him (see Philippians 3:9).

What you need to see throughout this passage is that Paul gladly left behind his pursuit of superstardom in Judaism because of his passion to know Christ with the kind of intimacy that transcended every other relationship.

This brings us to Philippians 3:10. If you need a verse to build your life around, this is it. If you want a pursuit to focus the rest of your life on, there's no better one than this. "That I may know Him and the power of His resurrection and the fellowship of His sufferings, being conformed to His death."

Victorious Christians know Christ more intimately.

We know about resurrection power. It's the power that raised Jesus up out of the grave. Now let me ask you. What problem or need do you have that resurrection power can't handle? What is dead in your life that needs resurrection? When you make intimacy with Christ a priority, you tap into this power.

Paul once made a very interesting statement in regard to his knowledge of Christ. The apostle said, "Even though we have known Christ according to the flesh, yet now we know Him in this way no longer" (2 Corinthians 5:16).

Before his conversion, Paul knew about Christ in the sense that he had heard about this Man Jesus and perhaps had even seen Him once. But after becoming a Christian, Paul truly came to know the Lord, and his previous casual knowledge was erased because he became a brand-new creation (see v. 17).

What happened to Paul was a genuine "power encounter." He came face-to-face with resurrection power. When you know Christ, the old stuff is erased. No wonder the apostle said, in effect, "Out with the old knowledge. I've found the new!"

Why is it that some Christians have victory while others are defeated? The answer isn't in their circumstances, because victorious Christians and defeated Christians face basically the same kinds of trials. The answer isn't in who goes to church more often or who reads the Bible more.

The answer is that victorious Christians know Christ more intimately, and thus experience His resurrection power.

A lot us would like to put a period after the phrase "the power of His resurrection" in Philippians 3:10. But if we are going to know Christ with the kind of intimacy that draws us close, we must know Him in "the fellowship of His sufferings, being conformed to His death."

We are called to share in Christ's sufferings. For most of us, that simply means standing up for Christ even when someone at work is making fun of us. For Paul, fellowshiping with Christ in His sufferings meant severe persecution, numerous hardships, and finally martyrdom. But it also meant a special kind of intimacy with the Lord that can't be known any other way. If you have ever suffered deeply with another person, you know what I'm talking about. We'll never be truly intimate with somebody else if we say to that person, "I only want to share the good times with you. Keep your suffering to yourself."

THE ADVANTAGE OF INTIMACY

Lois and I have been married for more than thirty years now. When two people share their lives for that long, they come to know each other so well they begin to anticipate each other's thoughts. Many times we say the same thing at the same time, or one says just what the other is getting ready to say. We joke about it, but it's part of the beauty of intimacy.

It really disturbs me when people come to see me and want to get divorced after they've been married only six months or a year. They usually say something like, "We didn't know marriage was going to be like this."

Of course not. They haven't been married long enough to know what marriage is like because they haven't had time to develop real intimacy.

Falling in Love with Jesus

So many Christians want to know the five things they can do to achieve spiritual victory or the four steps to peace. That's the American way. Just give me a list of things to do, and I'll knock myself out doing them.

Don't misunderstand. Nothing I am saying about performance-oriented Christianity is meant to imply that we don't have to do anything as Christians. God has prepared us to do good works (see Ephesians 2:10). And there may well be four or five things we could either stop doing, or start doing, to strengthen our walk with Christ.

The problem is that we attribute to our lists a power they don't have. Suppose a Christian brother says to me, "Tony, give me a list of five things I can do to be a better Christian."

So I give him a list of the basic stuff like reading his Bible and spending time in prayer, and then I call him two weeks later to see how it's going. "Not really any better," he tells me. "I already knew about the things on the list. I just can't seem to pull them off consistently."

This imaginary brother's problem is our problem too. We know what to do. The issue is where we get the power to do what we know. The Bible says the power comes in the relationship. Fall in love with Jesus all over again, and you won't need anyone to keep reminding you how important it is to read God's love letter to you or spend time communing with Him in prayer.

Stepping Out from the Dead Folk

Paul was not only ready to identify with Christ in His sufferings, but also in His death (Philippians 3:10).

Let's do a quick refresher. Part of our new identity in Jesus Christ is identifying with His death (see Romans 6:1–6). When Jesus died, we died with Him to the old fleshly way of life. But, praise God, that's not the end of the story. When Christ got up out of the grave, we got up with Him! Paul said his goal in identifying with Christ was "in order that I may attain to the resurrection from the dead" (Philippians 3:11).

That sounds like Paul was talking about the resurrection at the end of time. But there's more here than that, as wonderful as that is. Stay with me, because this is sweet.

It doesn't show up in the English text, but there's a prefix attached to the word *resurrection* that literally means "out of resurrection." Paul wanted to be resurrected out of something. What was it?

We could translate this "the resurrection out from among the dead." Paul wanted to be so alive in Christ that when he walked around among spiritually dead people who did not know God, the life of Christ would be pulsating through him with such power that it would be clear to everyone this guy was really *alive.*

Why did the shadow of Peter passing over sick people heal them, and why did his chains fall off in prison (Acts 5:15; 12:7)? How was he able to praise God for the privilege of suffering for Christ (Acts 5:40–41)? Because Peter met Jesus in a new way at Pentecost in Acts 2. Peter knew Christ in the power of His resurrection and the fellowship of His sufferings.

When I was a boy in Baltimore, the fire department would come around on Saturday and open the fire hydrant to bleed the line. The water would gush out, and we would get our shorts on and play in the water.

But I couldn't understand how all of that water could come from that little pipe. So one day I asked my dad about it. He explained that the hydrant was connected to an underground pipe that led to a reservoir. As long as that connection was in place, plenty of water would be coming out of the pipe.

If there is no water of life gushing out from you, you don't need a bigger pipe. You need to fix the connection. You need something inside that connects you with the power source.

To put it another way, God only feeds hungry people. If you are not hungry to know Him, put this book down right now and pray, "Lord, make me hungry for You. Give me a passion to know You that exceeds my desire for anything else in this life."

THE PRODUCTIVITY OF INTIMACY

We said above that pursuing intimacy in our relationship with Christ does not mean a do-nothing faith. On the contrary, one of the most intimate passages in all of the Bible teaches what I call the productivity of intimacy.

Staying Attached to the Vine

Jesus spoke the words in John 15 in the Upper Room just before His crucifixion, probably the most intimate setting we are told about in Scripture. With His disciples close around Him, and John leaning on His breast (John 13:23), Jesus said, "I am the true vine, and My Father is the vinedresser. Every branch in Me that does not bear fruit, He takes away; and every branch that bears fruit, He prunes it so that it may bear more fruit" (15:1–2).

Jesus used a familiar illustration to make His point. The disciples knew all about vines and fruit. Notice Jesus' emphasis on the productivity of their connection to Him.

Being a Christian isn't just hanging onto Jesus, drawing life from Him, and not producing anything. Even productive believers undergo pruning to increase their fruit-bearing.

So the disciples knew right away that Jesus expected them to be productive. The question was, how were they to produce the fruit that God desired?

Jesus continued, "Abide in Me, and I in you. As the branch cannot bear fruit of itself unless it abides in the vine, so neither can you unless you abide in Me. I am the vine, you are the branches; he who abides in Me and I in him, he bears much fruit, for apart from Me you can do nothing" (John 15:4–5).

God wants us to be productive, but He doesn't expect us to produce our own fruit. The key is in our connection to Jesus, the Vine. As branches we *bear* fruit, but the life-giving substance flows to us from the Vine. Anytime we try to produce fruit on our own, it's going to be from the flesh and, therefore, rotten fruit.

The difference is very practical. When a Christian husband tells me, "I don't love my wife," he is saying that in his flesh he can't produce real love for his wife, and I would agree.

But that's not the issue. The issue is, Can Christ love this brother's wife through him? The answer is yes, because love is a fruit of the Holy Spirit. The only question is whether this husband is willing to be a productive branch, allowing Christ to produce His love through the husband for his wife.

Taking Away the Struggle

Abiding in Christ is another name for intimacy with Christ. Christ wants to express His life through you, which comes through your attachment to Him. Intimacy with Him means productivity.

If your prayer life is just a matter of shooting up panicked "911" emergency petitions when you're in trouble, you're missing this intimacy. If you have your devotions in the morning so you can get them out of the way and get on with your day, you don't understand abiding. If church is just your weekly "nod to God," you won't bear fruit.

Abiding means just what it says. It means to remain, to stay, to keep the connection strong. It's a very freeing way to live, because it means you can take a deep breath and just get to know Jesus. It takes away all the self-induced struggle.

A young woman in our church, after years of smoking, decided she wanted to kick the habit. She tried every stop-smoking product on the market, but nothing worked. Finally, she decided that instead of focusing on all the things she was doing to quit smoking, she would focus on being in God's presence and getting to know Him. Within thirty days, she had quit smoking because of the power of the Vine.

The story is told that a bulldog and a poodle were arguing one day. The bulldog was making fun of the poodle, calling him a weak little runt who couldn't do anything.

Then the bulldog said, "I challenge you to a contest. Let's see who can open the back door of their house the fastest and get inside." The bulldog was thinking he would turn the doorknob with his powerful jaws and open the door, while the poodle was too small even to reach the knob on his back door.

But to the bulldog's surprise, the poodle said, "I can get inside my house faster than you can. I accept the challenge."

So with the poodle watching, the bulldog ran to the back door of his house and jumped up to the doorknob. He got his teeth and paws around the knob and tried to turn it, but he couldn't get enough of a grip on the knob to turn it. He finally had to quit in exhaustion.

Now it was the poodle's turn at his back door. "Go ahead, you little runt," the bulldog growled, trying to soothe his wounded pride. The poodle went to the door and scratched a couple of times. The master not only opened the door, but lovingly picked the poodle up in his arms and carried him inside.

The difference was in the relationship. Some of us are bulldog Christians. It's all grunting and growling and trying, when Christ wants us to come close to Him.

THE PROCESS OF INTIMACY

The title of this section may sound unusual, because intimacy seems like one of those things that should just happen spontaneously, without any real direction.

Wrong. Ask any married couple if deep, satisfying emotional, spiritual, and physical intimacy happens magically, with no effort on the part of either spouse. It doesn't work that way.

There is a process to intimacy with Christ, and we read about it in Matthew 11:25–30. Jesus issues an invitation to intimacy, but it's only for certain people, and it involves a definite process.

For Dependent People Only

In Matthew 11:25, Jesus prayed, "I praise You, Father, Lord of heaven and earth, that You have hidden these things from the wise and intelligent and have revealed them to infants."

Why did the Lord preface His invitation to intimacy with a statement like this? Because God does not reveal Himself to the proud and the self-sufficient, but only to the humble. Anyone who thinks he is smart enough to fix his own life isn't ready to admit his need and draw close to God.

But babies are helpless and totally dependent on their parents. Babies can't do anything themselves. All they can do is cry out in need and wait for someone to help them. To those who recognize their need for God, Jesus makes this invitation:

> Come to Me, all who are weary and heavy-laden, and I will give you rest. Take My yoke upon you and learn from Me, for I am gentle and humble in heart, and you will find rest for your souls. For My yoke is easy and My burden is light. (Matthew 11:28–30)

Talk about intimacy in a relationship. You can't get much closer to another person than being yoked together.

Harnessed Together with Jesus

But Jesus' invitation raises a question. How can He talk about yokes and loads, which suggest hard work, and about rest in the same breath? To most of us, rest means kicking back in the recliner. But that's not the kind of rest Jesus was offering.

A yoke, of course, is a harness that goes around the necks of two oxen so they can pull a load. Accepting Jesus' yoke is a picture of submission to Him, but it's also a picture of help because you're not pulling the load alone. Jesus is yoked with you, and He's going to take the lead.

I've heard that in each team of oxen, one is clearly the leader and the other follows. Jesus will do the work and take the lead, but we have to be yoked to Him to get the benefit.

So to enjoy intimacy with Christ, you have to bow your head before Him and be willing to accept His yoke. Jesus promises that because He is gentle and humble, His yoke won't choke you. It won't be wearisome or confining or constricting to you. In fact, the irony is that if you want to be free at last, allow yourself to be yoked to Jesus by submitting your will to His.

In verse 29, Jesus promised rest to those who submit to His yoke. In the previous verse He had said, "I will give you rest." But then He said, "You will find rest." What's the difference?

If you have come to Jesus Christ as your Savior, you have been given rest. It's called peace with God, meaning your sins are forgiven and you are no longer an object of God's wrath.

It's possible to have peace *with* God and yet not have the peace *of* God, which is that ongoing sense of assurance you have when you are in intimate relationship with Christ. Jesus said that only comes as you "learn from Me" (v. 29).

It's also possible to accept Christ's yoke and then start fighting and pulling against it when your life doesn't seem to be going in the right direction.

But peace and rest come when you truly relax in the yoke and let Christ lead the way. The Christian life is supposed to be a life of rest. Not laziness, doing nothing, but resting even in a yoke as you are joined in intimate relationship with Christ.

One day my car started sputtering and acting funny, so I had to pull off the road. A person can get very dirty and sweaty messing with a car, and I was dressed in a suit. I didn't know what to look for under the hood, anyway.

But I was able to stay cool, because I had a card in my wallet that signified a very important relationship. It was my membership card in the American Automobile Association (AAA).

I just picked up my phone and made a call, and a wrecker came and yoked itself to my car. I sat with the driver as he towed my car where it needed to go. I didn't have to do anything except admit my helplessness, call for help, submit to the "yoke" of the wrecker, and then rest in the help that was provided.

That's what Jesus Christ wants to do for you when you come to Him with your need. When you are willing to be yoked with Him in intimate relationship and fellowship, you'll find "soul rest" (see v. 29), which is a different kind of rest.

Soul rest means that when you ought to be shaken up over your circumstances, you're calm. Soul rest means that you're at peace when you ought to be going crazy, and sound asleep when you ought to be tossing and turning all night. Soul rest is what Jesus is offering you and me today if we will make knowing Him the passion of our lives.

Chapter Thirteen

THE BEAUTY OF BROKENNESS

Our world doesn't put much value on broken things. A culture that worships youth, strength, outward appearances, and self-reliance doesn't see any beauty in brokenness.

Our culture sometimes even discards broken people. If a baby in the womb has a defect, abort it. If an adult's body is broken by disease, help that person commit suicide. And if an elderly man or woman is broken by age and suffering, hide that person away. We don't want to be reminded of our frailty.

The world is scared to death of broken things, but I want you to know that God finds beauty even in brokenness. For a plant to rise from the soil, the seed must be broken open by the substance inside. For a baby chick to experience life, it must break the egg that surrounds it. Even to enjoy the fragrance of a perfume, we must break the seal on the bottle that holds it.

Complete humility before God is another form of brokenness that He values, and that's what I want to consider in this chapter.

Spiritual brokenness is so crucial that if we want to see God's face, if we want to be truly free in Christ, we must be broken first.

Let me begin by defining brokenness so you don't get the wrong idea. Simply stated, brokenness is the work of God by which He strips us of our pride and self-sufficiency so that the beauty of the life of Christ will shine through.

I wanted to get that definition down on paper right away, lest you think that being broken necessarily means experiencing some horrific catastrophe that brings you to the brink of ruin. I can't say what circumstances or people God will use in your life to bring you to the point of total dependence on Him, and we are all different in the way we respond.

The fact is that many people have suffered catastrophes without drawing any closer to God or even acknowledging Him. The issue in brokenness is not so much the circumstances, but our response to what God is teaching us through the circumstances He allows to come into our lives.

Having said this, though, we do need to realize that the Christian life is not a child's party or a perpetual hallelujah festival. True brokenness is God striking a blow at the flesh in such a graphic way that we have no strength left to fix ourselves.

When God blocks every exit you thought you could take to get out of your situation and you come to see that He and He alone is your resource, you are on your way to being broken and making the radical discovery that when God is all you have, He's all you need. The Bible teaches that God's power and presence are reserved for those who have given up trying to do it themselves.

THE PRINCIPLE OF BROKENNESS

The biblical teaching of our need for brokenness is not an easy word to talk about with you, because brokenness is not the path most of us want to take to find God's power and presence. But it is the path of God's choosing.

Dealing with a Serious Affliction

You may be wondering at this point why every Christian has to experience this breaking we're talking about. It's because whether we realize it or not, we are all afflicted with a self-sufficiency that creates a hard shell around us and prevents the life of Christ from shining through in its fullness.

This self-sufficiency is part of the fallen, sinful humanity we inherited from Adam, and it clings to us even after salvation because it is embedded in our flesh.

We are raised to be self-sufficient. We glory in our independence, which may be acceptable to people but is horrific before a holy God. We said in the previous chapter that God doesn't give His best to arrogant, self-reliant people who figure they're smart enough to make it on their own. God is looking for people who are humble before Him.

God keeps Himself distant from proud, self-reliant people.

We've examined this matter of living a liberated, empowered, Christ-centered life from a number of biblical perspectives. My sincere prayer is that something I have said in this book has given you an intense desire to know Christ above all else.

But I wouldn't be giving you the whole story if I didn't tell you that when you ask God to reveal Himself to you in all of His power and glory, you are asking Him to break you.

Someone may say, "Being broken doesn't sound very pleasant to me, so I'm just going to lie low and take the easy path." Well, that may help a person avoid being broken, but I wouldn't count on it. God may jolt that Christian out of his complacency. The Bible is replete with the reality of brokenness, this humbling activity of God by which He strips us of our self-sufficiency. Let me cite just a few examples.

"The Lord is near to the brokenhearted and saves those who are crushed in spirit" (Psalm 34:18).

"The sacrifices of God are a broken spirit; a broken and a contrite heart, O God, You will not despise" (Psalm 51:17).

"For though the Lord is exalted, yet He regards the lowly, but the haughty He knows from afar" (Psalm 138:6).

"For thus says the high and exalted One who lives forever, whose name is Holy, 'I dwell on a high and holy place, and also with the contrite and lowly of spirit in order to revive the spirit of the lowly and to revive the heart of the contrite'" (Isaiah 57:15).

"To this one I will look, to him who is humble and contrite of spirit, and who trembles at My word" (Isaiah 66:2).

The evidence is in, and it reveals that God keeps Himself distant from proud, self-reliant people, but draws close to the humble and broken.

Changed from the Inside Out

Since our sinful human tendency to self-sufficiency forms a hard shell around us, God must penetrate that shell in order to bring us to the point of utter dependence on Him.

In 1 Thessalonians 5:23, we find a clue to the method God uses to break open this shell. "Now may the God of peace Himself sanctify you entirely; and may your spirit and soul and body be preserved complete, without blame at the coming of our Lord Jesus Christ."

When God says He wants to sanctify us entirely, that's another way of saying we need to be totally transformed. Sanctification is simply the theological term for the process of spiritual growth by which God progressively makes us more like Jesus Christ. It begins the moment we are saved and will continue until the day we die.

What God is doing with us is transforming us *from the inside out*. Please notice that according to the verse above, this is exactly the order of the transformation. That is, God's transformation begins inwardly, in our spirits, and then proceeds out from there to our souls and our bodies.

This order is all-important, and it fits with a key principle of the liberated Christian life that we have been running into throughout this book. This principle is that outward performance alone will never get us to where God wants us to be, because we will never be able to please God by performance alone. Do you see how Paul reinforced that truth in 1 Thessalonians 5:23? The body, representing our outward actions, comes last in the order of transformation for a very simple reason I'll illustrate once more.

The problem with a thief, for instance, isn't in his hands. The problem is in his mind or spirit, which is telling him that stealing is OK and ordering his hands to steal. Transform the spirit, and the hands will follow. Otherwise, you can handcuff a thief and take him away, but he's still a thief inside.

Too many Christians want to get victory over bodily sins and bad habits of the flesh without being truly transformed within. But God starts with the spirit because our spirit is the portion of our being that makes us conscious of God. When God breaks us and sets us free in our spirit, then our soul by which we are conscious of ourselves and our body through which we are conscious of the outside world will fall in line.

Bucking and Kicking All the Way

If you're a parent, you know how different your children are in the way they respond to discipline. One child will collapse in tears at the slightest word of rebuke, whereas another child will buck and kick like a wild bronco at the rodeo.

Paul was definitely in the latter category before his salvation. God had to ride Saul of Tarsus like a wild, bucking horse until Saul was literally facedown in the dirt. Up to the moment of his conversion, Saul was a self-righteously smug, independent operator doing his "persecutor of Christians" thing. But the moment Saul met Jesus, his independence ended and he became totally dependent on the Lord. To reinforce to Saul the reality of his new dependent status, God struck him blind for three days, and he had to be led by the hand (see Acts 9:8).

You and I need to know that God will do whatever it takes, for as long as it takes, to bring us to the point of true brokenness so the life of Jesus can break forth from us. We can help determine how long the process takes by our response, or resistance, to the process.

Our church in Dallas operates a Christian school. We decided at the beginning that the school would enforce a dress code by requiring the students to wear a uniform. Any Fellowship Christian Academy student is identifiable by his or her uniform. It's required if they want to be part of the program.

The students may not always like the color or style of the uniforms, and they may not always think they look good in them. But all of that is really irrelevant if they want to attend our school. If a student says, "No uniform for me; I'll dress any way I want," that's fine. That student just won't be part of the program.

We've been dressing ourselves for too long spiritually. We're used to putting on what pleases us and what we think will make us look good to others. God wants us to put on Jesus Christ and make Him our new "look." However, before we can be clothed with Christ, God has to get us out of the old rags.

THE PROCESS OF BROKENNESS

The principle of brokenness has a process associated with it. God has a means to break our self-sufficiency so He can teach us the lesson Paul learned: "My grace is sufficient for you, for power is perfected in weakness" (2 Corinthians 12:9).

Before we look at the process, I need to correct a very common misconception. Most Christians have made this statement at one time or another: "God will never put on us more than we can bear." That's not necessarily true.

I know this idea comes from 1 Corinthians 10:13, which says God will not allow us to be tempted beyond what we are able, but will give us a way out of the temptation. This is an ironclad promise, because temptation to sin is not from God. It is not His will that we be overwhelmed by the devil's ploys.

But when it comes to trials and discipline from the Lord, there is at least one occasion in which God will put more on us than we can bear, and that's when He's trying to break us.

We have big recycling bins on our church property that collect paper, glass, and aluminum. The purpose of recycling is to give old bottles and cans new life, but to do that the old products have to be broken down to their basic components.

This is accomplished with fire so intense that the glass or aluminum is melted down so it can be reshaped into something brand-new. God will keep us in the fire as long as it takes to burn away the old self-life and reshape us (2 Corinthians 1:8–9). The Bible indicates that He will use at least three things to break us.

God Uses Satan to Break Us

One means God uses to break open our shell of self-sufficiency is the devil. Satan may be a roaring lion, but he's a lion on God's leash.

The patriarch Job is the classic example of the way in which God permitted Satan to afflict one of His children until Job was brought to a place of complete helplessness. There is a lot of this we don't fully understand, but I want to look at the back end of the process and what Job said at the end of his ordeal, after God had also examined him through a series of penetrating questions (Job 38–41).

We often forget this part of the story. Everyone knows that Satan put Job through some of the hardest trials ever recorded in the Bible. But God was in control of the situation, not Satan. The devil was merely God's instrument.

When it was all over, Job said to God, "I have heard of You by the hearing of the ear; but now my eye sees You; therefore I retract, and I repent in dust and ashes" (Job 42:5–6). We need to read this statement in light of what the Bible says about Job right at the beginning. "That man was blameless, upright, fearing God and turning away from evil" (Job 1:1). God even repeated the same commendation of Job (see v. 8).

What was going on here? Why did a righteous man like Job need to be broken? It wasn't necessarily because he did anything wrong. Job wasn't perfect, but there is no indication that Job's trials were a discipline for sin.

You need to keep this in mind, because when we use the word *discipline* to help the process of brokenness, we aren't saying it's always a punishment for sin.

If Job was the most upright person on earth, why wasn't he exempted from being broken? Because God wanted to take Job deeper than he had ever been before, and Job himself said the result was so awesome that it was like meeting God for the first time after only hearing about Him.

Let me put this contrast in today's terms. A believer might say, "I go to a good Bible-teaching church with my Bible under my arm. I can quote Scripture. I pray and read God's Word every day and give a regular tithe.

"But now that the Lord has broken me, it's as if all my previous Christian experience were just the prelude to this." Job didn't say, "God, it's great to see and know You in a new way. But it wasn't worth all the pain." No, Job fell before God and repented of ever questioning His care and goodness.

You see, we want to argue the theological ramifications of the way God used Satan to break Job. But we have to let the two principal characters in the story, God and Job, have the last word. God said, "I am the eternal God, and I am your God." And Job said, "O Lord, I thought I knew You before. But I am overwhelmed by Your awesome presence."

God Uses Sin to Break Us

Well, if you can handle the fact that God may use Satan to break us, you won't have any trouble with the fact that God also uses sin to break us. God never endorses sin or encourages sin, just as God never endorses Satan. Sin is always a bad investment because we reap what we sow, but if we insist on sinning, God can turn our sin around to accomplish His purpose.

Jacob was a cheater and a con artist who deceived his father, Isaac, and stole his brother Esau's birthright. Then Jacob had to do what a lot of con artists have to do when their scam is uncovered. He had to hit the highway. Jacob was away from home for years, but he was still pretty much the same schemer at heart until God broke him, quite literally, in a nighttime wrestling match (Genesis 32:22–32). The result of the match was that Jacob finally gave up his scheming ways.

David's great sin with Bathsheba was a breaking point in his life, and in reflection David wrote Psalms 32 and 51.

God used the sin of Moses to strip him of his self-sufficiency. Moses decided he would deliver Israel from Egyptian bondage on his own, so he went out ahead of God and wound up killing an Egyptian (Exodus 2:11–12). Moses then had to flee and spent the next forty years in the desert learning what he could not do on his own. In fact, he learned the lesson of self-*in*sufficiency so well that he didn't think he was ready when God called him forty years later. During those four decades, Moses moved from self-sufficiency to insufficiency so that God could become his sufficiency.

Peter's denial of Jesus is probably the most vivid New Testament example of the way God uses sin to break His people. Pete's threefold denial was bad enough, but he made it worse by playing "Mr. Self-Sufficient." He even sniffed at the other disciples for not having the stuff he had. "Even though all may fall away because of You, I will never fall away" (Matthew 26:33).

Jesus set Peter straight, but I love what else Jesus said to him. "When once you have turned again, strengthen your brothers" (Luke 22:32). Jesus was saying, "Peter, you don't know what you are saying. I know you are going to sin and fail Me, and it will be a very painful, breaking experience for you. Satan wants to crush you, but once you have been broken you will be ready to be the leader I called you to be."

I need to remind you how low Peter had to go before he was truly broken. He not only denied Jesus three times, but he left the disciple business and returned to fishing. Jesus met Peter at the seashore and forgave him three times before Peter was ready to shepherd God's sheep (John 21:15–17).

God Uses Circumstances to Break Us

God can also use circumstances to break us.

I recall the story of John Mark, a young disciple in Jerusalem who thought he was ready for the ministry. He packed up and came with Paul and Barnabas to Antioch, and then he went with them on the first missionary journey (Acts 12:25; 13:5).

But it got tough out there, and John went back home (Acts 13:13), no doubt a broken young man who had probably decided he would never have what it took for ministry.

Later, as Paul and Barnabas got ready for their second trip, they disagreed so strongly over John's fitness for ministry that they separated (Acts 15:36–40). Barnabas gave John a chance, and he responded so well that near the end of Paul's life, one of the people he wanted around him was John (2 Timothy 4:11).

You may encounter any kind of trial in the process of being broken, but don't mistake the hand of man for the hand of God. Let me explain what I mean. God may have intentionally allowed that person, that problem, or that situation to achieve His will. Trying to run from problems by changing jobs or spouses may take you from the proverbial frying pan into the proverbial fire.

Sometimes God wants us to hit rock bottom so we will discover that He's the Rock at the bottom. He will do whatever it takes to bring us to the place of brokenness.

When I was a kid, I had one of those classic piggy banks with the coin slot in the top. When I wanted to get money out of the bank, there was only thing I could do—turn it upside down and shake it hard. I did a lot of shaking because there was something of value inside that I wanted to bring to the outside.

God does the same thing with us. We have a great treasure inside us, the life of Jesus Christ. But that treasure is encased in a hard shell that hides it. So God has to shake and strip us to bring the treasure out.

THE POWER OF BROKENNESS

At first glance, the terms *power* and *brokenness* don't seem to go together. Certainly the world would not put these two concepts together. But in God's kingdom, what the world thinks is normal is often turned upside down.

That's the way it is with the spiritual discipline called brokenness. As we noted earlier, the path to power with God is the path of brokenness. We may draw back from the idea of God breaking us, but when we are broken before Him we will see God's power in our lives in a way we never thought possible.

A Reason for the Thorn

We don't always know the reason for our trials, but God revealed to Paul the reason for his "thorn in the flesh" (2 Corinthians 12:7). God sent it after giving Paul a vision of heaven (vv. 2–4), something no other human being had ever seen. Paul explained that the thorn was "to keep me from exalting myself" (v. 7). Paul may have been to heaven and back, but God wanted to keep him from becoming self-reliant or self-sufficient because of what he had experienced. Any tendency Paul would have toward pride was erased by the humbling affliction of this thorn.

What happens when you get a long, sharp thorn in your flesh? It hurts, and it will continue to hurt until you pull it out. It will also cause you grief as long as it is in your flesh because your clothing will snag and pull on it and cause further pain. If the thorn is big enough, and sunk deep enough into your flesh, you will basically let everything else go while you focus on removing this painful irritation.

The Bible never says what Paul's thorn was. This is intentional because God wants this to apply to any thorn in your life—anything nagging you that you can't get rid of. Paul prayed three times for God to remove the thorn (2 Corinthians 12:8). But God had another plan. He wanted to keep Paul dependent by leaving the thorn in, so the apostle would learn both how great God's grace is, and how great His power is when we allow Him to totally strip away our self-sufficiency. God is at His strongest in us when we are at our weakest.

Examples of Power in Weakness

The Israelite judge Gideon learned that principle during his great victory over the Midianite army (Judges 7–8). Gideon faced an army of 135,000 troops (Judges 8:10) with 32,000 men, but 22,000 left when he offered them the chance.

But God wasn't satisfied yet. All but three hundred men were finally weeded out of the Israelite army, and the ones who were left attacked the Midianites with lamps and trumpets and defeated their army.

Back at the beginning of the story, God told Gideon what He was doing. "The people who are with you are too many for Me to give Midian into their hands, for Israel would become boastful, saying, 'My own power has delivered me'" (Judges 7:2).

We talked earlier about Jacob and his wrestling match with God. Jacob left that match physically weak and broken, but he had a changed heart and new power with God.

The psalmist said, "It is good for me that I was afflicted" (Psalm 119:71). After Moses was thoroughly broken by God in the desert, he appeared before the most powerful ruler in the world, performing unbelievable miracles and demonstrating God's power in a way that could not be missed. Moses demonstrated that "[God's] power is perfected in weakness" (2 Corinthians 12:9).

If You Don't Have the Power

It's possible that you are reading this and thinking that while all of these stories about God's power are great, there must be something wrong in your life because you aren't experiencing God's grace or seeing His power the way Paul described.

Paul didn't experience power until he saw suffering as a gift.

In many cases, the problem is that we only read the first half of Paul's statement in 2 Corinthians 12:9. The idea of surpassing grace and power is great, but the apostle had more to say. "Most gladly, therefore, I will rather boast about my weaknesses, so that the power of Christ may dwell in me."

This is the tough part, because most of us have to admit that our version would read, "I will rather complain about my weaknesses, so that the power of Christ may not dwell in me."

When Paul discovered that God had all the grace he needed for his affliction and that God's power was tied to the thorn, Paul responded, "Bring on the thorn! I even praise God for it, because it is bringing me God's grace and power." Paul went from praying for deliverance to thanking God for the thorn.

If you have a thorny person in your life from whom you have prayed to be delivered, and God hasn't delivered you, maybe He wants you to experience His grace and power through dealing with that person. But you won't experience the grace and power until you move to praise.

Paul praised God for the most irritating, painful reality in his life—a real "sacrifice of praise to God" (Hebrews 13:15). That sounds wonderful, and we sing a worship chorus today about bringing a sacrifice of praise into the house of the Lord.

But, you see, a sacrifice means that something had to die on somebody's altar. That's important to remember, because only dead people get to see God's face. If you want to see God in terms of seeing His surpassing grace and power, you have to die to your own sufficiency. That's why Jesus' call to discipleship is to deny ourselves and take up our cross, an instrument of death.

There's nothing wrong with asking God to remove your thorn. But when your prayer for deliverance turns to praise for your problem, you're on your way to power, because God is going to give you grace.

God's program of bringing us to brokenness doesn't include room for complaining. Paul didn't experience power until he saw suffering as a gift. He concluded, "Therefore I am well content with weaknesses, with insults, with distresses, with persecutions, with difficulties, for Christ's sake; for when I am weak, then I am strong" (2 Corinthians 12:10).

You only discover that Jesus is all you need when God has stripped away your self-sufficiency and brought you down to the bare bones of life.

A furniture refinisher usually starts by using strong chemicals to eat away the old varnish or paint. Then the piece is sanded down to prepare it for the new finish. That's an easy process to describe, but it's painful to undergo when the recipient of the stripping and the sanding is you or me.

We pray, "Lord, this thorn is painful." God says, "I know, but praise Me because My grace is sufficient."

"But, Lord, it hurts. It hurts!"

"I know, but don't complain. The pain is necessary to bring out the full beauty of Christ in you."

And all of a sudden, that beauty bursts forth and we see what God is making out of us. Our identity in Christ begins to reveal itself, and we find power we never had before, because we have been broken.

Have you ever prayed, "Lord, break me in order that I might know Your surpassing grace and power"? It's not an easy prayer to pray, but realize that your loving heavenly Father only breaks to remake. He only strips away the old to reveal the beauty of the new.

If you want to know the fullness of Christ, you need to experience the beauty of brokenness. God has an amazing ability to take our trash and turn it into His treasure.

Chapter Fourteen

FREE AT LAST

One of the great contradictions of the American experience is that so many colonists who fought long and hard, and sacrificed so much, to be free of British tyranny, themselves enslaved Africans and defended slavery.

Free people owning slaves is not only a contradiction in terms, it's a contradiction in morality. The experience of slavery was so cataclysmic for America that the country could not survive without coming to grips with the issue and fighting a devastating civil war.

You see, when you find freedom, you ought to offer it to other folk too. When you're living as a free person, slavery ought not to be part of your vocabulary. If freedom is worth fighting for, and sacrificing everything for, then it's too precious a gift to deny to others by holding them in slavery.

What's true of human freedom is also true of spiritual freedom. So I want to conclude our study by sharing several encouraging biblical principles and issuing one more invitation to embrace and enjoy the freedom Christ purchased for you on the Cross. It's past time for us to live free in the Lord.

SET FREE TO SOMETHING BETTER

I mentioned before the problem that was common to so many newly freed slaves after the Civil War. They did not know where to go or what to do because slavery was all they had ever known.

These former slaves had lived under the old master for so long that they didn't know what to do with freedom. They may have been set free *from* something, but they didn't fully grasp the fact that they had been set free *to* something else. That's why some freed slaves simply remained on the plantation.

Leaving the Plantation

This problem is as old as mankind, because there has been some form of slavery since the beginning of time. Knowing how to make the most of freedom is a problem in the spiritual realm too, as evidenced by what seems to be a puzzling statement in Galatians 5:1. The apostle Paul declared, "It was for freedom that Christ set us free; therefore keep standing firm and do not be subject again to a yoke of slavery."

At first glance, it might appear that Paul is simply stating the obvious. But there's a principle here that has formed the governing thesis of this book. Let me state the principle in these terms: Christ did not pay your sin penalty on the cross and open the door to your prison cell of sin so you could just sit there and remain a prisoner to the world, the flesh, and the devil. True freedom is not just being liberated from something bad, but liberated to something better. People who don't understand what they have been freed *to* will wander around aimlessly, never really enjoying their freedom.

We've studied the situation in Galatia enough to know that this was far from a theoretical issue. Paul wasn't playing word games. He was trying to keep these believers out of the clutches of the Judaizers, who wanted to put the shackles of law-keeping on God's people. Paul had to tell them, "Don't let yourselves be put back in bondage."

For us as Christians, freedom includes being set free from anything that would prevent us from experiencing God's will—another name for God's best—in our lives.

And lest anyone think I am advocating that we throw off all restraints and all rules, let me reaffirm one last time that freedom in God's kingdom is not the absence of rules. No one can enjoy freedom without legitimate restrictions. A fish is free to roam the ocean, but not free to roam the forest because it is not equipped to live outside the realm of water.

So why doesn't a fish protest this restriction and try to wriggle up on land? Because God has provided everything it needs in its legitimate environment. We could say that by putting a fish in water, God set that fish free *from* dying on land and set it free *to* enjoy life to the full in the water.

This "to-from" principle means we should never say, "Thank You, Lord, for freeing me from the shackles of sin," without saying in the next breath, "and thank You for setting me free to know and do Your will for me."

Tired of Being a Slave

Do you know why some Christians are not truly free in Christ? Because they are not yet really tired of their slavery to the flesh and the devil. They're like the prisoner who is released but then goes right out and immediately commits the same crime that put him behind bars in the first place.

But a released prisoner has another choice. He can cherish and protect his freedom by turning away from that which held him in bondage and living like a free man. That's what he was released to do in the first place. The warden could say to this prisoner, "You're being set free to stay free. Don't go back to your old crowd and let them mess up your freedom."

COMING OUT OF THE CELL

So if Christ set us free so we could stay free and enjoy freedom to the full, how do we become free at last?

Well, when the door to your prison cell swings open and the

guard says you're free to go, the best thing you can do is get up and walk out of that cell and never look back.

If what I have said has helped you to better understand the extent of what Christ did for you by living a sinless life, dying on the cross, and rising the third day, then this book has accomplished one part of its purpose. Christ did not liberate us so that Satan and our sin-contaminated flesh could continue to boss us around and keep us tied to the old plantation.

Trying to Free Ourselves

But there is another purpose for this book that I hope has been accomplished under the Holy Spirit's guidance: to set you free from the futile attempt to achieve your freedom by your own efforts.

Paul said it in no uncertain terms: "*Christ* set us free." He did not say that Christ merely gave us the opportunity to set ourselves free. As the old hymn says, "Jesus paid it all."

This is such a liberating concept because it doesn't matter what has been holding you in bondage to the old way of life. It doesn't matter how strong the influence of sinful patterns and old habits may be. It doesn't even matter how deep the wounds of past hurts may be. Jesus can break every chain because it is for freedom that He has set us free.

But this also means we have to give up our self-effort of trying to please God and live free. You've probably seen pictures of modern prisons with thick doors on the cells instead of bars.

Imagine a prisoner beating on one of those doors with his hands, trying to get free. When the guard asks him why he's doing that, he says, "I'm trying as hard as I can to get free." It will never happen.

But when someone pays that prisoner's debt to society and opens the door, that prisoner can walk free. Sin had locked us up behind the prison doors of guilt, shame, and deception. But Jesus served our time for us, and we can now go free.

Past Time to Be Free

The Emancipation Proclamation that declared an end to slavery in America was signed by Abraham Lincoln on January 1, 1863. The official end of slavery came almost three years later when the thirteenth amendment to the Constitution was ratified on December 18, 1865.

For some us, it has been two years, ten years, or even twenty years since our freedom was declared, and we're still not really experiencing it.

The problem could be that like the slaves after the Civil War, we're afraid of the risks associated with freedom. As terrible as bondage was, at least the slaves knew they had food and a place to sleep on the plantation. The unknown must have seemed pretty frightening compared to the known.

That's just how a lot of the plantation owners wanted it. They wanted their slaves to feel so tied to the plantation that they were not willing to leave and attempt to live free.

Jesus Christ is the Liberator who has freed us from our shackles. But Satan is the plantation owner, whispering in our ears, "You'll never make it out there. You've been here so long this is all you know. At least here, you know what to expect."

But with Christ, the risks of freedom are really no risks at all. How can it be a risk to commit ourselves totally to Someone who gave up heaven to save us and set us free?

MAINTAINING YOUR FREEDOM

So your freedom in Christ is a gift of God's grace that you can do nothing to earn by your own effort. But that doesn't mean you have no part to play in living free. There are some things you can do to maintain your freedom.

Watch Out for the Enslavers

The fact that Paul warned the Galatians, "Keep standing firm and do not be subject again to a yoke of slavery" (5:1), reminds us that there are always people around ready to enslave us. Let me show you several examples.

Paul began his letter to the Galatians by warning them, "There are some who are disturbing you and want to distort the gospel of Christ" (1:7). This problem was so serious that the apostle continued, "But even if we, or an angel from heaven, should preach to you a gospel contrary to what we have preached to you, he is to be accursed!" (v. 8).

Satan and his forces are ultimately behind every effort to distort the gospel of God's grace and bring believers into bondage. Elsewhere Paul teaches that we shouldn't be surprised that the devil gets religious to try to enslave us. "Even Satan disguises himself as an angel of light" (2 Corinthians 11:14).

We have noted that the church in Galatia was being troubled by "false brethren" (2:4) who wanted to put these Christians into the shackles of law-keeping. Don't be shocked when people who pass themselves off as servants of God use the Bible to try to mislead God's people and bring them into bondage to some man-made scheme. They'll come right to your door to do this.

Other people will try to enslave us, but we can also put ourselves in bondage by putting ourselves on a performance basis with God. Don't let anyone rob you of your liberty in Christ. "Keep standing firm" in your freedom.

Don't Make Yourself at Home

The actor James Dutton was in prison at one time before he turned to acting. One day an interviewer asked Dutton how he avoided becoming a repeat offender and going back to jail. Dutton's answer was very informative. "Unlike other prisoners, I never decorated my cell."

In other words, James Dutton never allowed himself to feel at home in prison. Too many Christians are not only in spiritual bondage, but they've also decided that since they aren't ever going to get free, they may as well make themselves at home. They resign themselves to living defeated Christian lives.

Help Others Enjoy Freedom

A lot of people and things can keep you bound, but once you experience true freedom in Christ there is nothing like it. You don't want to go back, and you want to help others get free too.

One of the best ways you can maintain and nurture your spiritual freedom is to help set other people free by refusing to hold them in bondage to your expectations and your preferences.

Christians need to put up a few yield signs along the way as they travel. You know what a yield sign means. It means you slow down and allow the other person the right-of-way so he can proceed to where he's going.

People's eternal destiny is not decided by the pastor's dress style.

The reason I say this is that many of us are too quick to impose our rules and our way of doing things on other believers. We need to give each other some freedom—not to sin, but to work out our own salvation with fear and trembling (see Philippians 2:12–13). I'm talking about letting people be who God called them to be, while simultaneously encouraging and correcting them when needed along the way.

The church is not an assembly line or a cookie cutter, stamping out each person in exactly the same shape. Many issues of the Christian life are nonessentials, meaning they aren't vital to the core of our faith.

Worship style is one of these issues. Some people prefer their pastors in long robes, while others are more comfortable in a church where the pastor wears slacks and a shirt with no tie. These are matters of preference in which we need to give others some freedom. People's eternal destiny is not decided by the pastor's dress style.

I like what Paul said about these things. "Now accept the one who is weak in faith, but not for the purpose of passing judgment on his opinions" (Romans 14:1). Then he gave the example of a person who felt free to eat meat that might have been offered to a pagan idol, and the person who avoided meat altogether for fear of eating religiously "contaminated meat."

Paul's point was that each group should avoid condemning the other. Then he gave a definitive principle. "Who are you to judge the servant of another? To his own master he stands or falls; and he will stand, for the Lord is able to make him stand" (v. 4).

If I could paraphrase Paul's message in today's terms, it would be "Back off. Give others some slack. They're serving Christ, not you, and He can take care of them."

Again, this is not about giving people the choice of whether they believe Jesus Christ is the Son of God or allowing people to sin freely with no attempt to correct them. Paul was referring to personal preferences and convictions.

We would have a lot more peace in the body of Christ, and more believers discovering their freedom, if we spent less time trying to make other people like us. I need to encourage others to pursue the Lord, even as I pursue the Lord myself. If we do that, we'll be going in the same direction. The Lord can take care of changing us where we need changing.

So while you're standing firm in your freedom, don't pull the ground out from under other believers who are trying to stand firm in their freedom.

THE MECHANICS OF YOUR FREEDOM

What do I mean by the mechanics of freedom? Well, the mechanics of something means the way it works, what makes it go.

There is nothing mysterious about the mechanics of discovering, enjoying, and maintaining your freedom in Christ. It can be summarized in the single word *grace.*

The Amazing Nature of Grace

I've been preaching the grace of God for more than thirty years, and I'm just now beginning to discover the richness of this word. That's one reason I wanted to write the message of this book for you.

Grace means that God does it for me and through me and in me, rather than me trying to do it myself. And I have a never-ending supply of grace because God's grace will never fail.

We've spent a lot of time in the writings of Paul, the apostle of grace, so it's appropriate that we turn to Paul to grasp the greatness of grace. For this, I want to look at Paul's personal statement of what grace meant to him:

> For I am the least of the apostles, and not fit to be called an apostle, because I persecuted the church of God. But by the grace of God I am what I am, and His grace toward me did not prove vain; but I labored even more than all of them, yet not I, but the grace of God with me. (1 Corinthians 15:9–10)

To those who questioned how a persecutor of Christians could qualify to be an apostle, Paul would respond, "I agree. There's only one reason I'm here. It's by grace."

Paul wasn't just being humble here. He went on to say that because grace involves responsibility, he labored mightily out of gratitude for the great mercy God had shown him in Christ. Paul looked at his former life and what God had done for him, and he said, "How could I not live to please a God who poured His grace out on me?"

But just to make sure no one charged him with pride, Paul added, "No, it wasn't me doing it. It was the grace of God working in me." You see, when believers live by grace, no one has to beg them to serve or give. People who have to be begged to serve God or support His work aren't living by grace.

Keep Heading Toward Freedom

So if grace is the mechanism that keeps our freedom in Christ running and gives us the power to go, how do you keep the mechanism of grace operating?

You get up every morning and thank God for your freedom. You get up every morning and continue your journey from the plantation of your former slavery to free territory. You don't look back, but keep pressing on in freedom.

You say, "But how do I know I can make it? I've been on the plantation so long. Freedom looks so risky. I'm afraid to step out and live the grace life, because I don't know where this journey is going to take me."

If you're feeling uncertain or afraid, let me leave you with a benediction:

> Now to Him who is able to keep you from stumbling, and to make you stand in the presence of His glory blameless with great joy, to the only God our Savior, through Jesus Christ our Lord, be glory, majesty, dominion and authority, before all time and now and forever. Amen. (Jude 24–25)

Are you afraid you won't be able to keep yourself on the path? You've got it. That makes you a candidate for grace. Are you afraid you'll stumble? You will, on your own. But the issue of being free at last isn't about you or me; it's about Christ, the One who can keep us from stumbling.

GOING BACK HOME

The story is told of a father who had five sons. The first son was obedient, but the other four were rebellious boys.

This family lived near a river with a powerful, dangerous current, and one of the father's standing rules was that his sons were not to play in this dangerous river. But the four rebellious sons decided they didn't have to listen to their dad, so they went into the river one day and were soon swept away by the powerful current.

Mile after mile these four sons were carried downstream by the river, until they were washed ashore almost dead many miles from home in a rugged wilderness area. They were hopelessly lost and disoriented.

The brothers built a fire on the riverbank and sat around the fire talking about how good they had it at home and how they wouldn't be in this mess if they had just listened to their father. But none of them knew how to get back home.

After a while one son said, "I'm going to build myself a hut. It's obvious that I'm not going home anymore, so I'm going to make the best of it right here. This is my home from now on."

The second son said to the first son, "I'm going to go with you and watch everything you do, and when I get back home I'm going to tell on you. I'm going to tell Dad how you forgot him and forgot your home and decided to stay where you were. I'm going to report everything I see."

The third disobedient son said, "Well, I'm not going to sit around here. I want to go home, but I'm going to make it on my own. I'll do whatever it takes to get home, even though I don't know the way by myself." With that, he got up and disappeared into the thick wilderness, clawing and scratching through the bush in a desperate attempt to save himself.

The fourth rebellious son was deeply sorry for what he had done. Yet he also knew his father loved his sons and would send help to find them. So he stayed by the riverbank, watching for the rescuers he knew his father would send.

Sure enough, after the brothers had been stranded for some time, the son who hadn't disobeyed his father came down the river in a boat, looking for his four rebellious brothers. He saw the repentant brother standing on the riverbank waving his arms.

The good brother pulled up in the boat and said, "Dad sent me to find you and bring you home. I have everything we need to travel back upstream and go home. But where are our other three brothers?"

The repentant brother showed him the hut that the one brother had built. The rescuing brother knocked on the door and said, "I've come to save you, Brother. Come on, it's time to go home."

But the "hut" brother said, "No, this is my home now. I've been away from my father's house so long this feels like home. Thanks, but I'm staying here."

So the rescuer went to the second stranded brother and told him it was time to go home. "I'm not leaving until he does," he said, pointing to the brother in the hut. "I'm going to watch everything he does so I can report him to Father when we get home. If I leave, there won't be anyone to keep an eye on him."

The third brother was already long gone by this time. He figured that if he made it home the hard way by trying to do it all by himself, his father would see how hard he had worked and love and appreciate him more than if he took the easy way.

So the only brother left to rescue was the one who was willing to go home the father's way. Even though the father had sent his good son to bring everybody back home, only one of the four rebellious brothers made it home.

The first of these rebellious sons was unwilling to take the risk of making the trip home. He was more willing to live in a hut than to face uncertainty in getting back to the father.

The second son was so focused on somebody else's sins he forgot it was his own sin that got him in trouble in the first place.

The third son was a do-it-yourselfer. He believed that if he tried hard enough and clawed his way along, he could make it home on his own.

Only the fourth rebellious brother understood that the sole way to get out of the mess he was in and get back home was to follow the son sent from the father.

Which of these four sons are you most like? God the Father has sent Jesus the Son to locate His brothers and sisters and bring them home. There is joy, ample provision, and freedom in the Father's house. Don't let anyone or anything keep you from following the Son of God to freedom.

CONCLUSION

When America's soldiers came home in 1945 after World War II, there was great celebration. When the American hostages came home from Iran in 1981, there was great celebration. When the Berlin Wall was torn down in 1989, there was great celebration. And when Kuwait was liberated by the troops of Desert Storm in 1991, there was great celebration.

Nothing produces celebration quite like the knowledge that you are victorious, that the enemy has been defeated, and, therefore, that you are not subject to the enemy's bondage anymore.

Since this is true, you should be shouting in celebration right now. Why? Because as a new creation in Jesus Christ, you are free. You are not fighting *for* victory but from a position *of* victory. And if Christ has set you free, you are really free.

As we have seen, the Enemy does not want you to learn and experience the truth of your identity in Christ. He wants you either to dismiss it or to relegate it to the category of what is often called "positional truth," with no day-to-day reality attached to it.

But one of the best ways to be reminded of your freedom in Christ is to celebrate it each day. Praise God daily for the freedom Christ has given you because of your identity with Him. Praise Him for your freedom whether or not you feel it emotionally right now, because it's true!

And since Satan and his minions are allergic to praise, they will have to leave you alone when you praise God for what is true, rather than believing the devil for what is a lie.

When you celebrate your freedom day in and day out, claiming God's grace to make the fact of your freedom your experience of freedom, then you will be able to sing the refrain of the old Negro spiritual: "Free at last, free at last. Thank God Almighty, I'm free at last."

SUBJECT INDEX

SCRIPTURE INDEX

Moody Press, a ministry of Moody Bible Institute,
is designed for education, evangelization, and edification.
If we may assist you in knowing more about Christ
and the Christian life, please write us without obligation:
Moody Press, c/o MLM, Chicago, Illinois 60610.